Equipotential Space

FREEDOM IN ARCHITECTURE

Equipotential Space

FREEDOM IN ARCHITECTURE

Renato Severino

PRAEGER PUBLISHERS

New York • Washington • London

PRAEGER PUBLISHERS

111 Fourth Avenue, New York, N.Y. 10003, U.S.A.
5 Cromwell Place, London S.W.7, England

Published in the United States of America in 1970
by Praeger Publishers, Inc.

© 1970 by Praeger Publishers, Inc.

Library of Congress Catalog Card Number: 70-124863

Printed in the United States of America

Acknowledgments

I began writing this book, while living in Rome, because I hoped by analyzing the ideas set forth here in light of my professional experience and my search for a new perspective to clarify them for myself.

These pages were completed in New York, where I now live and work. I feel it is possible today only in the United States to foresee a prospect for architecture in Western culture.

Exhaustive analysis of phenomena is necessary in the search for new paths, as is objectivity in order to avoid questionable and hasty conclusions. In this laborious process, I have had the invaluable aid of many friends, both in and out of the academic world. I am grateful to them for encouragement in my research, for acceptance or rejection of my beliefs, and for stimulating discussions of my theories. Their constructive and enlightening criticisms have prevented this book from becoming too personal an account and have helped to make it instead, I hope, a contribution understandable to all.

I am especially indebted to Professor Mario Salvadori, Chairman of the Division of Architectural Technology at Columbia University, for the many and varied contributions he has made to my thoughts, as both a scientist and an art lover. I am confident that with his encouragement the school will make significant progress in devising new means of industrialized construction.

For help in my research, I extend sincere thanks to Kenneth Smith, Dean of Architecture, and Romaldo Giurgola, Chairman of the Division of Architecture, and to the students of the Division of Architectural Technology at Columbia University.

The staff of Urban Technology International deserves particular mention for its fundamental assistance in the form of ideas and hard work. Anne Gottlieb, William Clark, Steven Winter, William Kennedy, and Melanie Modesitt were especially helpful in putting together this book and, in the process, formulating the working principles of Urban Technology International.

I wish to thank Marcello Indiati, senior partner of Comtec, in Rome, for contributions based on his extensive and creative business experience. I would like also to include an appreciative mention of the staff of Comtec, with whom I worked for many years on projects for African and European countries: first of all, Bruno Conti, senior partner; Marino Rossi, Nanni Pazzi, Nora Masi, Roberto De Rubertis, and Fabrizio Vescovo, architects; Fernando Conti, Lorenzo Lanari, and Massimo Tessitore, engineers; Mario Recchia and Cesare Urbani, graphic designers.

I also wish to thank my good friends Alberto Spreafico and Francesco Alberoni, both eminent sociologists, and Chiara Briganti, architect.

Ana Roigt Loud's views on contemporary culture provided indispensable assistance, as did the clear and pragmatic contributions of Raleigh Chaffee.

Marianne Clark did a splendid job on the initial editing. John Dixon, senior editor of *Architectural Forum*, gave me moral and professional support. His professional honesty and the equilibrium of his critical judgement have contributed a great deal to these pages.

Brenda Gilchrist, Matthew Held, and Ellyn Childs of Praeger Publishers deserve mention for their excellent work in putting the book together. Paul and Barbara Bodin are responsible for its fine artistic layout.

Finally, I want to thank my wife, Mimma, for her help and interest throughout the writing of the book.

New York, New York
July, 1970

Contents

All the buildings and designs illustrated by photographs and drawings are original works of the author.

Equipotential Space

FREEDOM IN ARCHITECTURE

Introduction

As man enlarges his world, both physically and socially, its problems as well as its benefits assume greater dimensions. The medium of technology has also grown, keeping pace with this change of scale, and has, in its turn, changed our world. We are all aware of the presence and power of technology as an inescapable fact of life; its power and range are unique and unprecedented. Today, technological growth seems irreversible. The need for it exists and is acceptable in all sociopolitical systems.

Why, then, is there such widespread fear and distrust of technology? Its benefits are so taken for granted that we describe our miseries in terms of the lack of them. Those applications of technology which we tend to remember seem to be those which were at first most controversial. Technology has been accused of destroying both nature and man, of poisoning spirit and flesh.

The Western world is heir to two compelling and sometimes conflicting ideas: The uniqueness of each man, and the common humanity of all men. From the idea of uniqueness, we gain our concepts of art, freedom, personal belief, and free will; from the idea of humanity, our beliefs in democracy, equality, and our recognition of the most pressing needs existing in the world today.

It is only through the power and prevalence of technology that the desired quality of responses to problems can be produced—and in the quantity required by humanity. Technology has multiplied our capability. Through technology in architecture, both art and humanity can be combined.

In this book, we explore the possibility of quality in quantity—in architecture. There are many contradictions inherent in this possibility, and many different answers.

In a world arriving at an unprecedented state of mass consciousness and oneness and at the same time viewing life in pairs of extremes—have/have-not, rich/poor, progressive/reactionary, black/white—the power of technology to reach all men and give them a standard in common makes it the only medium that will enable us to give an effective answer.

Independent of our volition, a new architecture, one

that uses technology as a basic tool, is in the throes of being born. This book is an attempt to sketch the outline of a new process in an interdisciplinary vision that, while it may often be simplistic and incomplete, deals with the factors out of which we shall build our future.

Experts in political science, sociology, anthropology, and psychology may take issue with certain assumptions or statements in these pages. We are very anxious to have their reactions but are, above all, anxious to enlist their deeper participation in architectural problems.

Our commitment is based on this new process, in which architects will see their moral purpose. In a mass-produced architecture, the challenge is to defend freedom of expression and the right of people to shape their own environment. As always, architecture will express in physical terms this dimension of freedom.

I.

Architecture as a Cultural Function

Present Inadequacy of Cities · Historical Survey · Limitations of Modern Movement

In this century, architecture has become expressive of the divisions among peoples. It has become a vehicle for discrimination and has been used to impose the will of the few upon the many.

It appears that today architecture is considered less and less necessary and is used, if at all, as a cosmetic. Because architecture is costly, it is often misunderstood, even by the class that claims it as its province. Architecture has become an elite upper-class process in a world that is urbanizing dramatically and that no longer considers the upper class a relevant source of direction.

Unlike cars, boats, and electrical appliances, the quality of whose function and design constantly improves, architecture has not yet become available to a consumer market.

Recently, architects have tried to meet mass problems through Utopian planning projects. Unfortunately, these are only giant versions of limited, personal statements. The effort has been made to incorporate the community through scale alone. This is the typical error of the artist-architect confronted with a world that can no longer be enclosed and contained by one person's horizon. We can no longer afford this individualization.

Architecture will have failed if it is unable to meet the challenges of modern society. As an art, it is in danger of falling into the lamentable position of an archaic institution artificially preserved. Although the processes of architecture continue, they lack relevance. This is apparent in the failure of architects to cope with the urban crisis.

Our cities no longer correspond to our way of life. Originally, cities were organized as administrative bases for agricultural and mercantile systems. They were developed by an elitist society in which the largest sector of the population contributed little consumption, service, or movement. We continue to use the same planning principles today because we have not successfully adapted urban plans to a democratic society which is industrialized, and physically and socially mobile. As a consequence we are beset by disunity, decay, and discomfort.

A city should be and, until now, has been more than an aggregation of buildings. Yet the modern urban environment has become just that. Buildings sit in so many rows, with only superficial consideration for over-all spatial relationships, patterns of access, or human usage. Parts of the city are overused and over-developed, with consequent crowding, speculation, and pollution; other parts become slums, with the same results. In the absence of a totally usable city, many of its inhabitants move out to the suburbs, finding there a *petite malaise* instead of the great urban sickness.

The effects of both illnesses are well known: costs spiral; buildings both old and new deteriorate; the highways take over; breathing space is hard to find; the entire citizenry is oppressed. Today's architects are left to create settings for the affluent classes, sheltering them from the harsh realities. For the giant corporations and master developers, contemporary architecture adds style. It is not surprising, then, that architecture, relegated to these superficial activities, no longer bears major responsibilities for shaping society.

Architecture in the past has been recognized and used as an extraordinarily powerful social force; as a profession, it served the needs of society; as one of the arts, it expressed that society. This duality has given architecture a unique position, with power to move an idea from conception into concrete reality. The combination of these two facets—service and expression—into one function creates a dynamic that can shape a culture. Through the dynamic of architecture, ideals and goals become a pattern of unconscious, unquestioned reality. The fine arts have claimed this power, but their distance from the patterns of daily life has attenuated any such action. Architecture, with its intimate connections to these life patterns, constantly conditions people through the forms and spaces it creates for their daily use.

The entire tenor of life of certain cultures has stemmed from and been reflected in their architecture. When we look at the great pyramids, we can feel deeply the death-oriented culture of the ancient Egyptians and imagine the thoughts and the lives of men who concentrated so much effort on mortuary equipment. Or, looking at a great Gothic cathedral, we see again how men created a special kind of life for themselves by building monuments to their philosophy.

This power of architecture is an extraordinary one and, of late, little recognized. But it did not escape those who consciously fostered new cultural ideas. History abounds with examples of great men enlisting architecture to their service. Certainly the most straightforward illustration of this power of architecture is found in the actions of Louis XIV. Versailles was created in order to realize Louis' concept of absolute monarchy. Not only was Versailles' sheer magnificence of great political importance, extremely effective in aweing representatives from rival nations, but its size and plan also had their more domestic purposes. Louis used Versailles to vitiate the political power of the nobility. The palace life offered amenities unknown in the isolated fortresses that were the traditional homes of the nobility. Lured to Versailles by grace and beauty and kept there by honorary functions, the nobility were rigidly organized into a hieratic order that focused on and exalted the king. The nobles fought over location of their quarters and their court prerogatives instead of over taxes and land. Through the architecture of Versailles, Louis substituted etiquette for politics and anchored European culture in France for nearly two centuries. Absolute monarchy was realized because of Versailles, not merely symbolized by it.

In recent times, the importance of this working relationship between architecture and cultural direction was best articulated by the leaders of the Modern Movement—Walter Gropius, or even Frank Lloyd Wright. The Modern Movement was aware that society and architecture had become disjointed and that architecture did not relate to modern ways of life; it wanted to change the relationship of the people to their houses and their objects, of buildings to one another, of builders and techniques to buildings, of mankind to the city. Because of its efforts, our own notions of interior space are more fluid, less ritualized; our aesthetics less artificial, more open to our own experience; and industrial processes have become tools for creative work, not necessarily synonymous with shoddiness and vulgarity.

Nonetheless, the hard facts remain. The current architectural sterility comes about because the Modern

Movement merely changed façades. In basic ways, buildings of the Modern Movement are no different from those of the Renaissance. The relationship of an architect to his constituency remains the same elitist one. The relationship of buildings to one another as discrete entities remains the same. Basic proportions of space remain the same. The processes of producing buildings remain the same.

The Modern Movement has not changed the social sense, the spatial scale, or the urban nature of architecture. The Modern Movement has not been able to instrument its ideas about new relationships. The tremendous upheavals in the social fabric of the 1930's and the conservative reaction suggest that the time was not right.

The moderns, unable to accomplish their most basic goals, fell back on their sense of artistry. The new city of Chandigarh in India seems today to be a fine interpretation by Le Corbusier of the old town nearby. Mies van der Rohe's buildings are striking for their perfection of detailing. The only lasting effect of the Modern Movement's early impact has been the International Style of architecture, with its neat lines and emphasis on pattern.

The present difficulty of architecture is that, as the leadership of the Modern Movement passes away, the old goals are forgotten, the bitter struggle is put aside. The style they created is too alluring. We continue to develop their style, to refine façades, to engage in artful play. We cannot accept the failure of the Modern Movement or apply the principles of its pioneers to the problems that beset us still. We have inherited a style and betrayed a responsibility. Even as avenues of glass buildings continue to grow, the overwhelming problems of the rest of the city increase at an even greater rate.

II.
The Change of Scale: Challenge

Emergence of Mass Society · Growth of Technology · The Human Dilemma

The crisis of architecture has developed because of the tremendous change in social directions. For architecture to work in its most powerful way, a very delicate balance must be maintained between society's directions and the architectural dynamic. The power of architecture to shape a society cannot be imposed upon that society but must be integrated with it.

The present dilemma began when that delicate balance was upset, an upset precipitated by a tremendous change in the scale of forces in every contemporary phenomenon. This change of scale represents the very fabric of modern life. It is hardly surprising that man should be uneasy when he realizes that standard concepts of time, space, and social conscience no longer fit his world.

Mass society has been born. The entire world is demanding equality. For the comfortable and satisfied man, it is literally another barbarian invasion. The millions of people lacking housing, food, medical attention, and education will no longer tolerate the concept of a distant elite. In the heart of Western man, the fear of losing everything has to be balanced against his moral responsibility and human concern for suffering.

Above all, the emergence of a mass society means a tremendously enlarged need for architectural production, a need for millions of homes, schools, and hospitals. It is important to realize that sheer quantitative need, now of crisis proportions, has always existed. But there is a new qualitative need. Mass consumption is very different from mass existence. The new situation demands that architecture provide not for an elite but for the masses. At least two grave problems have arisen: First, how do you serve a client consisting of millions of people—how do you mutually decide what can be done? Second, how can any such tremendous need be met?

Historically, architecture has striven for the timelessness of permanence. Buildings were built, if not as monuments to immortality, at least to last for generations. The resulting environment—for those who possessed it—was one of security and solidarity. For the dispossessed, however, it was one of timelessness, in which improvement was imperceptible within any one generation.

That timelessness has been exploded. The self-satisfied man takes refuge in day-to-day living, the dissatisfied man is carried forward by his demands alone. There is little assessment or evaluation, and the lack of communication drastically limits the possibility of planning for the future.

The speed of change must become a continuum of events that develops a real and stable time dimension. It is only within such a dimension that an environment can be said to develop. Architecture faces the paradox of providing the security and solidity of the past and, simultaneously, of answering the pressing and rapidly changing needs of the moment.

Man's experience of space has also been subjected to tremendous change: Urbanization, more and more people compacting themselves into less and less space. Space in its former sense no longer exists. Room to spread out, to move about, to spare is simply an anachronism. Cities, by definition dense, are the dominant socio-spatial pattern, and their dominance is growing rapidly. Moreover, the advantages that attract people to the cities make it unlikely that this trend will be reversed.

But what about the monotony, the ugliness, the pressures of uncontrolled density? Anthropologists and psychologists concern themselves with the effects of density on the balanced functioning of human beings.

Urbanization presents a painful contradiction for architecture to reconcile. We want cities, but without the crowding and aggression inherent in their density. Planning can no longer be approached as a physical problem. We find ourselves unprepared to mediate between geometry and social science. Our task has changed from creating spatial forms to controlling density within forms.

The new necessities have become so urgent so rapidly that comprehension has been disoriented, incomplete, and, unfortunately, largely reactionary. The change in scale and its effects have been misunderstood as a disintegration of society. It has been called chaos. Not so. It should be seen as a nexus in which a synthesis of ideas can be developed until they become a dynamic force.

Ironically enough, man's ability to cope with the new

scale of the world simultaneously creates a still newer scale. Man's relationship to technology changes. The power of technology to change completely the shape of human life has become clear. Unfortunately, this power is clearest in its negative aspects. The point is not that technology is evil or has evil effects. We know that we cannot return to a pretechnological society. The difficulty is one of organizing a procedure for applying this awesome power to the service of human values.

Up to now, architectural processes have retained their essentially individual nature. Despite many efforts to apply the contemporary teamwork system to architecture, the design process remains isolated and personal. The product of design remains a specific building for a specific client. The building is produced by craftsmen as a unique object.

Our whole Western culture has been based on the possibility of individual action. No individual can oppose the enormous influence of technology. He is confronted, moreover, with social upheavals that previous processes do not enable him to control.

A common response to this dilemma is documented in cultural movements: existential literature and philosophy, the theater of the absurd, surrealism. Old goals are no longer relevant, it seems useless to formulate new ones. Western man no longer feels himself in control of his life.

A number of attitudes develop—privatism, hedonism, materialism, specialism—all different aspects of the same stasis of social responsibility. In short, the last quarter-century has been an amazing exercise in avoiding the future and the collective effects of our own actions. We have failed to face our responsibility for the endless proliferation of small wars, the racial conflicts, the poverty and degradation of man.

It is widely recognized that our society is at a turning point. The tenor of life will not remain the same. Two great forces—the change in scale and the power of technology—insure that in thirty years the world will be very different, virtually unrecognizable.

In the face of this prospect, mankind feels no security whatsoever. The range of predictions available to those who indulge in futurology is staggering. But there is one constant theme: technology. We know that our brave new world will be conditioned to its very core by technology. Over the past fifty years, technology has completely changed the ways in which we communicate, move about, preserve our health, keep house, dress, and entertain ourselves. Society is on the verge of revolution in the fields of education, production, and, indeed, genetic make-up. We stand in the same relation to the future as the Stone Age stands to us—with the exception that the tempo of change accelerates at a geometric rate.

Even with this certainty of technology and its progression, any extrapolation to the future from observations of contemporary society results in schizoid predictions. Schizoid because these divergent views are not derived so much from differing information as they are alternately equally strong—visions constructed from the same fact.

That fact is, of course, the application of science to our lives. At one point we are elated at the certainty of a life of gleaming, undreamed-of technological wealth, comfort, convenience, and achievement; the next minute, we are overpowered by an existence of relentless horror created by technological alienation, pollution, totalitarianism, and total annihilation. The dream or the nightmare? Each seems equally possible, even probable.

It is our paramount task to realize the dream. The attempt to deal with the two visions has led to a schizoid architectural process. Rarely dealing with technology and the future in a positive way and working to realize the dream, architects have more often reacted to the nightmarish possibilities. The struggle for both quality and quantity has disintegrated into isolated actions.

III.
The
Change
of Scale:
Response

Dichotomy of Quality and Quantity · Equivocal Position of Achitecture

The search for refinement independent of the needs of the society has weakened architecture. Quality architecture that fails to deal with the problem of quantity becomes a mere aesthetic play. This kind of response is based on the premise that housing projects or mobile homes are the uncontrollable result of the mass society—that the possibility of a quality architecture in a mass society would depend upon leisure, education, and financial means.

In architectural education, the refusal to face contemporary necessities has produced the most rebellious of all student groups. These students have realized that they are being systematically trained to a subordinate position, to powerlessness.

On the other hand, the response that emphasizes the quantity is becoming a vicious treadmill. The mass demand for a better life has been answered with mere quantity, stressing technology's power to turn out more products more quickly, more cheaply. But more of what? More slums? More shoddiness? More alienation? This approach confuses social responsibility with social engineering. And it intensifies the very totalitarianism and alienation it seeks to avoid.

These differing approaches—quality and quantity—could have produced a dialogue in which the interrelationships between the two concerns could be identified or could condition action. Instead, a truly schizophrenic loss of contact with reality has occurred and has produced a paranoid hostility toward integration of the two positions. So long as there is failure to grasp the unity of the problem, there will be a consequent aggravation of the situation—until, by default, the nightmare is reality.

It is this split that we feel as chaos and confusion. The underlying sense of powerlessness in the face of change of scale and the potential misuse of technology is at the basis of this division. True, the individual by himself can have little effect on these two phenomena. And, more importantly, the old processes, because they are essentially individualistic, cannot make this vital integration of forces and concerns.

Consequently, Western man has found himself growing more and more disengaged from his life, holding back his culture by clinging to old ways. This is certainly true of architects who have no guidelines for relating to forces that must be dealt with, and who hence have no means to achieve that delicate balance between dream and action so fundamental to the creation of a new environment.

IV.
The Image of the Future: Mass Culture

Necessity of an Image · Definition of an Image

A new architectural methodology must begin with a direction. In other words, precise, definite goals. The nightmare vision and even the dream vision that have been exerting so much influence are inadequate as objectives. It is imperative that we realize that what future we will have depends largely on what future we want. For both individuals and cultures, the image of the future is the sum total of their expectations.

An image of the future is not particularly important as revelation or as an intellectual construction; it is desperately important only in so far as it conditions present actions.

A vision of the future, either personal or collective, is a psychological fact. And, like any other psychological fact, it guides our action in certain directions. The future is not predetermined or out of our control or independent of man's action but is the result of man's reshaping his environment in order to reach certain goals—all according to his image.

Each of the major civilizations developed its own characteristic vision of the future. In fact, the history of culture is a history of images: Thinking about the future is recognized as a condition of survival.

It is the primary responsibility of any culture to cultivate an image consciously if it wishes to remain dynamic.

Lacking the driving force of a clear vision, modern Western culture stagnates between dream and nightmare, with nothing to pull it from the mire of present conditions. The image of a mass culture can provide the momentum needed to escape the current stagnation; it can heal the breaches that divide our actions; it can give us a perspective that utilizes the actual dimensions of life today, and an image of the future with legitimacy for all groups.

If a mass culture is the image of the future, architecture can form the environment according to that image and thus make mass culture a fact for all men. In working with the image of a mass culture, architecture can keep pace with social directions, instead of continuing its decline into irrelevance.

The means of achieving a mass culture is technology. With it we can begin to deal with some of the ideas that can help to resolve the current dilemma.

We may say, without much contradiction, that a Japanese camera or a German car can function all over the world, regardless of local social, political, or economic conditions. The same airplanes regularly serve all countries. Penicillin is equally useful for combating infections in India, Africa, and China, as well as in Europe. In these instances, a certain task has had to be performed, a certain standard of result has been expected, and techniques and equipment have been developed to provide widely acceptable responses.

These responses are products of technology. They begin with the assumption that all peoples of the world share samenesses, regardless of any local or historical factors.

This immediately relates to one of two working definitions of the study of culture: One is essentially the study of those elements of life that are shared among a group of people, therefore, of those things that are held to be the same. The second definition concerns what makes one group of people or beliefs identifiably different from any other.

In practice, both of these ideas have meaning and even coexist to some degree. On a world scale, technology relates to the first of these ideas and will be a tremendous force in shaping the mass culture. Technology, through its processes and products, is understood and held in esteem in both industrial nations and developing ones, by rich men and by poor. Technological products are mass artifacts, not only in terms of quantity but also in quality and economy. They provide a universal standard: All men relate to technology and, through it, to each other.

The antithesis of this relates to the definition of culture as differences among men. Opposing this process are the limited traditional attitudes derived from differences between groups or localities. These traditions will be referred to here as folklore.

Folklore tends to take an answer that worked yesterday and to enshrine it as valid for all time. It is a deification of a local status quo; it represents a static solu-

V. Technology as the Medium

Technology Versus Folklore · Universal Application of Technology · Technical Appendix

tion or a repeating answer and reduces responses to the level of predictability.

Folklore deals with personal images and comforting assumptions. The wish to prolong the present, no matter how bad, as a defense against an unknown tomorrow is hardly effective.

Architecture from now on must be totally integrated with technology, because that is the only medium that can be used to provide the necessary production levels in terms of quality, quantity, and economy. Technology is the *lingua franca* of the mass culture. That advanced technology can be applied to architecture has already been proven. European experience and recent American studies have shown that industrialized building technology can lead to higher quality, faster production, and reduced costs. Together, architecture and technology can give us the means to solve the problems of the city, not only in functional terms but also in realizing new and more meaningful ways of living.

The dynamic of architecture must start with housing. A change in a man's home will truly alter the way he lives and thinks more so than a change in his office or his school building. Technology and not folklore will enable all men to participate equally in the life around them.

Without technology, architecture cannot solve problems; neither can technology without architecture. In using a new image of the future, the dimension of the human values, of human responsibility, of imagination must not be neglected. The inclusion of this dimension must be assured. It calls for reintegration of values lost during the last century in the general split that developed between art and science. The industrial process constitutes that integration: the production system belongs to science, while the ideas belong to art. The two are united in the prototype, that is, in the materialization of the idea through the schematics of production. The industrial process moves from prototype to product. The prototype continues to advance—answering man's needs more precisely with a more advanced technology, continually improving and enlarging the product. In this process the costs diminish, assuring greater diffusion of the product.

The dynamic of architecture can create a material vision of the new way: it can build a prototype to influence other action, a social model in microcosm. Indeed, these possibilities can themselves become an image of the future, providing the power to meet contemporary challenges.

The following two buildings illustrate the point of the chapter. The first is a solution based on a folklore as a source of inspiration, and the second attempts to satisfy universal standards.

The Social Center of the University College of Cape Coast in Ghana was built in 1967 (*Figs. 1 & 2*). Housing student and faculty clubs as well as a cafeteria and shops, it can be considered a typical example of architecture in which forms prototypical of African folklore have been employed on a greatly increased scale. It is obvious, in fact, that the form of the main front of the buildings repeats the form of a mask, with the windows defined by means of slitlike apertures similar to those once used by local artists to draw together the parts of sculpted figures.

The acclaim that the construction enjoyed among European critics was not mirrored by the Africans' appreciation of this attempt to carry them back to their own traditions. The local people recognized certain functional features of this building, but they attributed no special value to the design that was worthy of future development. Their attitude is positive proof that the Africans, understanding that the new scope of their problems precludes a return to tradition, are seeking a different course along which to direct their culture.

As an attempt to understand cultures other than Western ones, modern, exotic, folkloristic architecture, such as the campus of the University College of Cape

Technical Appendix

Coast, is at best a weak first step against colonialism. At the same time, it and such other projects as Chandigarh by Le Corbusier and Dacca, Pakistan, by Louis Kahn are attempts via the Western approach to produce architecture in an exotic atmosphere.

All these solutions represent final expressions of elitist Western attitudes. They are badly received by the peoples of the areas; further, they are forever dated.

The eagerness on the part of the Third World to abandon its old traditions, use advanced technology, and adopt international ways of life testifies once more to man's desire to seek a common idiom.

An opposite kind of solution can be seen in a building constructed in 1960 (*Figs. 3–7*), which was planned as the prototype of a series of structures to be erected in various localities entirely by prefabrication. The building, a school for the children of Italsider Industries employees, was built in Piedmont, near Cesana Torinese, at an altitude of 5,500 feet. The design caused much apprehension because it appeared very different from other buildings, including modern ones, constructed in the mountains. Certain features—the roof with openings that permit sunlight to penetrate the building, and the construction, recessed into the land, encountered great opposition before the school was opened (*Fig. 6*). The concept of this school was an attempt to formulate a construction adaptable to no matter what climate or natural environment. For this reason, the building was designed in compact shape (180' x 180'), to avoid loss of heat in cold climates and yet to develop air currents within the internal space to permit easy cross-ventilation in warm climates. Moreover, the sixteen-foot projection of terraces around the entire construction protects the glass from the rays of the summer sun yet permits the more sharply inclined rays of the winter sun to strike the façades (*Fig. 7*). The continuous interior space, divided only by sheets of glass and curtains, allows the occupants to feel that they are together even while engaged in different activities (*Fig. 3*). In short, this building demonstrates that present-day technology is capable of producing solutions suited to any locality.

The limitation of the Italsider school is that it was considered only as a repeatable prototype, not as an expansible texture. In the future, buildings will have to be constructed of series of components that, when assembled, will allow for diverse and articulated spaces. It is unthinkable that they be conceived as closed and oriented forms, such as those of ships or automobiles, since that would preclude the possibility of integrating spaces on an urban scale.

1. Social Center of University College of Cape Coast, Cape Coast, Ghana. 1967. Views of model.

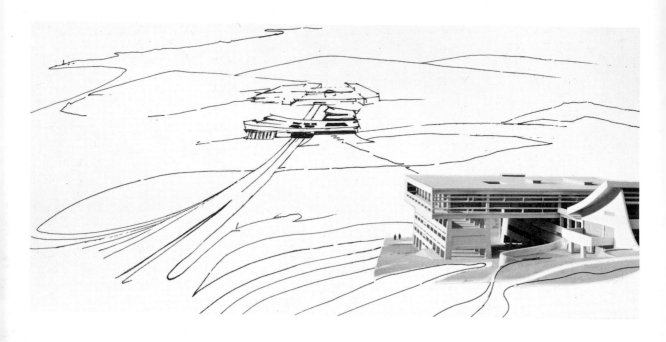

2. Social Center of University College of Cape Coast. The main staircase enclosure is shaped like an ancient African mask. The building is made of exposed reinforced concrete.

3

3–4. Italsider Resort School near Cesana Torinese, Piedmont, Italy. 1960. *3.* Interior. At each level, the internal continuous space is divided by glass partitions and curtains. The cylindrical core contains utilities and elevators. *4.* North elevation. The middle floor is totally fenestrated. The building was made of steel products available on the European market. It is an example of an "open system" design based on product performance.

4

5

5–7. *Italsider Resort School*. 5. View from east. The building is inserted in the ground. It consists of three floors plus a deck house. On the ground floor are situated the services; the middle floor contains teaching rooms and living rooms; the top floor contains the students' living quarters. *6.* Model. The roof of the building (approximately 180′ x 180′) is flat with open patios. 7. East elevation. Four bridges, on both the east and west sides, afford the eight independent groups of children a direct exit from the middle floor. The vehicular traffic at the ground-floor level does not interfere with pedestrians. Three feet of snow is usual in this area during the winter months, and temperatures in the summer often reach the 90's.

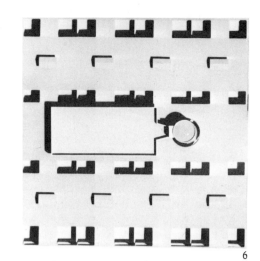

6

7

Our situation is this: We need millions of housing units, we need pervasive architecture, and we need both as soon as possible. This situation is world-wide. The Utopian nature of a house for a mass culture becomes apparent when one considers the range of socio-economic conditions existing in today's world. Because of these conditions, we cannot have the future we want now. But we will never have it unless we begin now to work for it. We need a standard that will be both the moral commitment to that future and the process for achieving it.

The standard is not frozen. It develops as choices are made among feasible courses of action. The responses possible in a rich country are widely different from those available in a poor one. These situations must be dealt with, not only in terms of products or definitions but also in terms of approach and effects. The extent of the supportable expenditure and the qualitative difference of needs—indeed, the entire range of socio-economic conditions—have previously suggested widely varying architectural and cultural approaches. Many people believe that these differences will remain relevant, that there must be many standards. Essentially, they believe that established cultural mores deny the possibility of an international culture and a standard based on total equality. Certainly such beliefs worked against any unity in the past and will remain significant in early stages of the new process.

However, as the standard of living becomes more and more a function of technology, it will become more and more feasible to formulate one international standard. The world-wide reaction to the technological process is making it increasingly evident that the needs, problems, and aspirations of all men are strikingly similar. As every part of the world struggles to industrialize and as the similarities grow, cultural differences are exposed as folkloristic.

Technology has already proven that medicines, cameras, and cars can meet one international standard, can be used equally well in different cultures. The same should hold true of housing.

Although the standard as a moral commitment demands a house for everyone, the process will take a long time. Three factors that will force the standard

VI.
The Dilemma of Standards: Quality in Quantity

Quality and Quantity ·
Toward an
Architectural Standard

to vary are magnitude, time, and money. It would be no great achievement to build two or ten or one hundred houses that satisfy the demands of the standards of a mass culture, but it would also be meaningless to build millions of dwelling units before an international approach is formulated.

The dilemma is the problem of developing a standard that can relate production, employment, and administrative programs to architectural and technical ones; the standard must adapt its processes to socio-economic differences without sacrificing or confusing its basic movement toward environmental equality for all. The standard must also consider the need for constant readjustments so that its own contributions can be taken into account.

This standard is based on the fact that industry today can plan and produce for a world-wide housing market, and such a development would certainly result in housing markedly different from that available today. A totally new way of living can be projected. The importance of the standard is that it is an architectural standard, not a survival device. A man living and producing at the level demanded by contemporary society certainly would expect and should have an environment in which he could provide for his personal physical and social needs as well as find a medium through which to participate. This, then, is the minimum requirement for the standard: A complete way of life should be defined in such a way that it becomes a usable concept in both rich and poor nations.

A standard in common means a shared understanding, a culture in common rather than a parity induced by force or by an action planned from the top.

The dream of many Western politicians has been to save the world from fear or to build the great society everywhere. However, these men have used their advanced technology more often as a medium with which to coerce rather than to build.

Nevertheless, it is clear now that technologically advanced arms are not adequate for the job of maintaining a society or protecting it from fear. While we are aware that the world is too large to be controlled by armed forces, it is not too large to have a standard in common among people.

The time is ripe now to initiate the study of a new methodology out of which will come new principles of architecture, not merely new techniques for producing shelters.

What we are really aiming for is a space for mass culture; a space in which all free initiatives of the society can survive and grow in an architectural milieu that reshapes itself accordingly.

VII.
The Solution: Equipotential Space

Methodology · Flexibility
and Continuity ·
Technical Appendix

In developing a new approach to deal with the problems described, we must clearly articulate a concept and begin applying and refining it on the level of the mass society. This concept is Equipotential Space. Spatial formulations in current usage proceed from a definition of space as a volume and are concerned with its geometrical characteristics. Instead, the definition could be extended to cover changing patterns of relationships. The matrix in which these relationships exist can be called Equipotential Space.

The determining characteristics of Equipotential Space are continuity, flexibility, and articulation. Instead of being planned for a few specific purposes, Equipotential Space can be modulated at will for any purpose.

Inherent in a model of this methodology are two independent and complementary subsystems, both of whose components are industrially produced. The components of the first subsystem define and structure the physical limits of a volume or territory in predetermined scale increments.

The components of the second subsystem provide the necessary environmental conditions and apparatus that allow these volumes to be used according to a particular program. We will speak of our methodology as a system of Equipotential Space and of its two subsystems as Frame Components and Function Objects (*Figs. 8–15*).

This methodology rejects building types—apartment buildings, office buildings, school buildings. Instead, it proceeds from a study of the functions that must be served by architecture. The activity volume of the structure creates space used to perform a task or service. The activity volume must be supported by smaller self-contained units for such functions as cleaning, cooking, washing, and resting, as well as those functions of communications, environmental control, and power supply necessary in all spaces planned for human use. In our solution, these small, self-contained units are referred to as Function Objects.

When the activity volume is defined by the Frame Components and the basic supporting functions are supplied by Function Objects, the flexibility inherent in Equipotential Space is achieved.

The only major difference among these Function Objects affects and is related to their scale and to the number of people who will use each simultaneously. Basically, there are two scales: that where functions are performed by no more than two or three people at the same time, and that at which many more people must be provided for. Essentially, functions are performed on the family level (*Figs. 13–14*) or the community level (*Figs. 8–12*). As the pressures of urbanization reduce the available space per person, Function Objects provide a more favorable ratio of activity volume to basic volume within any given space.

The most important characteristic of the Function Object is its mobility, which can be obtained with wheels or air-cushion devices. Mobility of Function Objects is the process by which total flexibility of Equipotential Space is achieved. It is, of course, faster and simpler to move a single object than a number of small parts, so long as the object and the means to move it do not become cumbersome.

Compactness, an integral characteristic of Function Objects, facilitates mobility and efficiency. With the decrease in available volume per person, the compactness of Function Objects is a space-saving device. Even a conventional small bedroom has wasted space that, using Function Objects, can be recaptured to make more spacious living areas. And, on a larger scale, rearrangement of living areas can be achieved by single actions instead of multiple operations—by moving furniture, moving partitions, changing lighting, or replacing furniture.

The enclosed nature of the Function Object is further indicated by the need to segregate these functions from activity volumes. The basic supporting functions must be enclosed in order to isolate noises, odors, heat, or provide for privacy.

Function Objects allow us to realize an adaptable and economical space. They provide for greater diversity of use and consequently greater utilization of a given area. They allow a total exploitation every day of every space, through mobility and interchangeability.

An example of the flexible use of space can be seen in any one of a number of public auditoriums where, rather than having four or five different specialized arenas, the changing of certain components allows, in one arena, for a track meet in the morning, a basketball game in the afternoon, a hockey game at night, and, the following day, for a theater performance. In terms of cost benefit, the most efficient use of volume and structure is achieved by making all the space work all the time.

The intent is there, the need for such flexibility is recognized. However, even in this case an arena has become a very specialized building type. Its equipment, for the most part, cannot transcend the set of uses for which it was designed.

Equipotential Space offers a possibility of real freedom. This is not freedom just to be different but freedom to participate as fully as possible, given social, economic, and technical reality. It is freedom to shape responsive solutions to immediate needs—and when these needs change, to have a new solution. The relative availability of options is a measure of the control man can exercise over his environment and therefore a measure of his relative freedom. In Equipotential Space, this sort of freedom can be available from the personal and familial levels all the way through to the socio-political level, all through the flexibility in shaping the space and controlling the environment.

The transformation of a space from one use to another can be most efficiently controlled through automated methods. The exact time and plan required for transformation would be readily available. A computer program could comprehend many factors, for instance, desirable room temperature at different levels of occupancy achieved by means of a few temperature-control Function Objects used temporarily to fill the need. This would end the installation of infrequently used permanent equipment. Such practices could achieve considerable reduction of capital investment, maintenance costs, and waste space.

As an exercise, it would be interesting to take an existing unit, such as a large urban university, that included (*Figs. 11–12*) almost all types of social activities on all varieties of scale, and conduct a use-study of all the separate, inflexibly defined spaces now existing, to find out what percentage of the time each space is being used. It would then be interesting to hypothesize the same events occupying the same time spans and relationships in an Equipotential Space and calculate the total volume required as a percentage of present supposed needs. Even with a finite, limited number of components within each subsystem, Equipotential Space can provide almost any variety of relationships (for example, space) required at any time. The standards of amenity are universal. The standards of use vary with the economic requirements of the individual or community; each programs its own solutions.

Equipotential Space is a new operational methodology for architecture. It completely changes the design, production, and utilization of buildings. In terms of the dynamic of architecture, the designer assumes a new position. He contributes the pieces that society as a whole and each individual can develop according to his own needs. It is paradoxical that Equipotential Space is both more designed and, simultaneously, less completely designed than conventional space. Function Objects and Frame Components are shaped by design and production needs and can be arranged according to the free choice of the individual. The result of this fusion of advanced technology and mass participation is the production of a continuous space, modulated over time to create a flexible living environment—together with all of the benefits of industrial standards.

The continuity of Equipotential Space exists in both volume and time. Applying its concepts, cities could no longer be divided into districts for purposes of exploitation, because the space would then lose its flexibility. Cities could not become obsolete, because they could constantly change to correspond to new situations. Articulation of space through Function Objects and Frame Components would make it both responsive and systematized. Quality would be inherent in the unity of the space and in the many aesthetic possibilities for arrangement of Function Objects. Quantity would be necessary in the industrial production of the components. This methodology would create the scale and continuity of the market required if assembly-line techniques were to be effective.

Equipotential Space develops a time dimension by relating objects and events in a volume over a period of time as needs change. One of the first and most important results of this kind of space is that it could destroy the stylistic differences among building types, and, therefore, the noncontinuous, decay-prone, egocentric cities of individual buildings would no longer exist.

A second immediate result would be the compacting and concentrating of our urban volume through a more efficient use of unit volume per unit time. The sprawl of urban and suburban wastelands need no longer exist, since we could adjust to changing patterns in a natural fashion, and there would be no cycles of speculation and abandonment. These changes could aid in recovering watersheds and open spaces, optimizing transportation, communication, and energy production, and, in short, allowing us to live with our technology rather than in spite of it.

Equipotential Space already occurs in an embryonic way in some current commercial construction. In a modern office building, the same basic volume can serve many different working situations, depending upon the environmental and architectural configurations chosen for it and its furnishings. This has led to the development of numerous subsystems—furniture, partitions, carpeting, and lighting—as well as mechanical and structural subsystems especially designed to permit maximum flexibility of the building volume. It is possible to imagine that within a few years the economic and social advantages of the total adaptability of Equipotential Space will be widely accepted in the market, to the extent that space in the new city will become an unlimited community utility. Anyone would then be able to find in the city a mode of arranging his own space within the context of the urban fabric.

Equipotential Space could be considered as Utopia in all but architectural terms. Criticism of solutions in Equipotential Space can no longer be only architectural but must be sociopolitical; it must be in terms of the real values of cities and not of cosmetic values.

Equipotential Space is a flexible environment for a free society. It is impossible to think of such a concept in a dogmatic regime in which everything is planned at the top. On the contrary, an Equipotential Space is made to contain all the forces in a continuously new balance, able to produce a sequence of solutions.

We want to describe a space capable of adapting itself to new equilibriums produced by the interaction of free activities—in short, a continuous readjustment between an individual's will and the available capacity for making it a reality in the shortest possible time. Large cities already live in a state of continuous disorganized mutation. Their increasing neurosis is due to the insufficient speed in putting thought into action. This process of constant change should not be obstructed if we believe that real actions must derive from changes in the status of our ideas. The continuation of Western culture is tied to this irreversible dynamic equilibrium. Mutation is our rule. Our happiness and our self-control are tied to the flexibility of a medium able to respond rapidly to our command.

Technical Appendix

Frame Components can be designed in many forms using simple or elaborate geometries, including organic forms, provided a flexibility of aggregation is possible.

To obtain this continuity in Equipotential Space, we must be able to join components of different systems, at least where different patterns meet. An "open" system in which different components can be inserted will not only be possible but more flexible—particularly in terms of marketing and construction operations.

Function Objects can be designed either as part of totally integrated systems or as separate entities to be used as free-standing elements. By producing them in closed systems, we can find specific geometrical relationships among related Function Objects.

Function Objects can be designed and produced in any form—even a completely spherical one (*Figs. 16–17*).

It will soon be possible to find on the market as many types of Function Objects as we have types of television sets or refrigerators today. They can also be custom built in limited series, and a great many inventions and solutions using advanced techniques and materials will be possible. Function Objects can be replaced, as today's electrical appliances are, as more advanced types or better designed ones are available.

Kitchen and bathroom design is becoming more sophisticated, as is the design of boats, cars, and office equipment. The traditional aesthetic models are no longer meaningful or relevant to the new technology.

Typical heights necessary for a certain number of people to communicate in the same space can be approached by establishing the minimum basic internal height of Equipotential Space. The level of communication intended allows people to see each other and to focus on one point in common. This situation will determine certain basic heights that can be, in this case (*Figs. 18–20*), 8 feet for 50 people, 17 feet for 500, and 35 feet for 10,000. The basic internal height will have to be defined in order to determine the modules in each of the Frame Components. The example shown here is no more than one possible solution.

8–10. *Equipotential Space.* 8. Example of the flexibility needed to achieve equipotential space. Function Objects—B (bath), K (kitchen)—can be moved horizontally on each floor of a building and vertically by elevators. 9. The positioning of two-story Function Objects by mechanical devices. 10. Plan of a composite Function Object accommodating locker rooms and toilets.

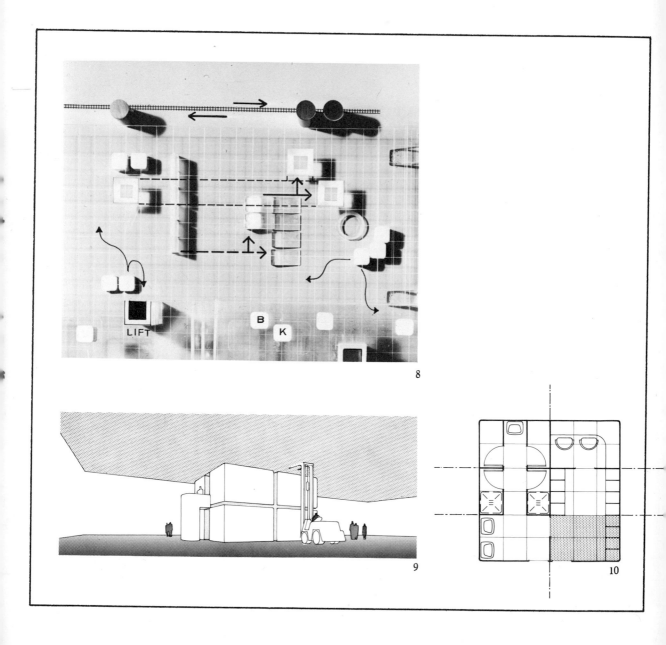

8

9

10

11–12. Equipotential Space. Examples of multi-purpose space in an urban configuration. The Function Objects can be moved from one area to another, enabling a variable number of people to perform different scale activities. The various Function Objects move along predetermined schemes: Air conditioners (*12*) move outside the building, and objects containing projecting apparatus and light equipment move along the ceiling of large assembly areas.

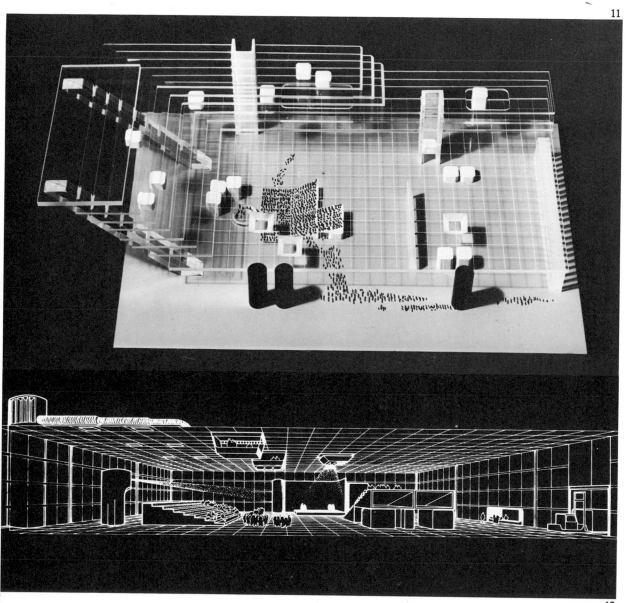

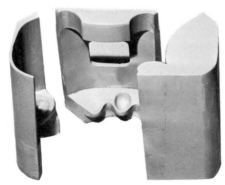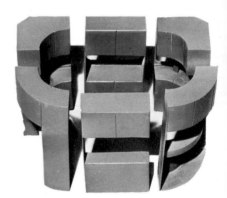

14a

14b

13

13–15. Function Objects. 13, 14. Examples of residential Function Objects. Function Objects can be of various shapes and can be made of several parts to achieve ease in transportation (*13*). The Function Object, two floors high, can be hung on the outside wall of the dwelling unit: kitchen and utility (K—U) and double bathroom (B—B). Free-standing bedroom (BR) can be moved in the internal space. Interchangeable components can be built to make bathroom (*14a*) and kitchen (*14b*) of different sizes. The bedrooms (*14c*) can be formed by a set of elements of different sizes. *15.* A space capsule is also a typical function object.

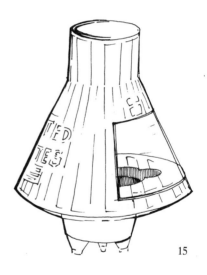

15

14c

16–17. Spherical Function Objects. 16. **Plan** (*a*) and sections (*b*, *c*). *17.* **View of model. The designer has a wide choice in conceiving forms of Function Objects. A kitchen can be designed as a sphere, adopting the diagrams of the most rapid and efficient use of utilities and storage space. A retractable table is contemplated as part of this design. Other operable parts, hinged to the main structure of the object, can be conceived to make its service more efficient.**

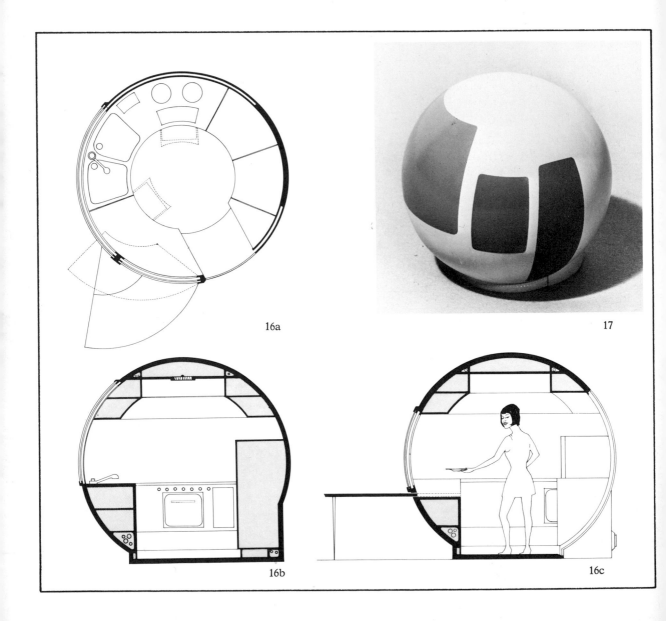

16a

17

16b

16c

18–20. Basic Heights. There are three typical room heights that can be assumed to be basic in determining the vertical module in Equipotential Space. Figure 18 represents the minimum height needed to accommodate up to fifty people (1, 2) in visual communication with a person situated in a focal point (3). The same situation is shown in Figures 19 and 20, but with the number of people up to 500 and 10,000 respectively. In Figure 20 there is the possibility of accommodating any indoor activity.

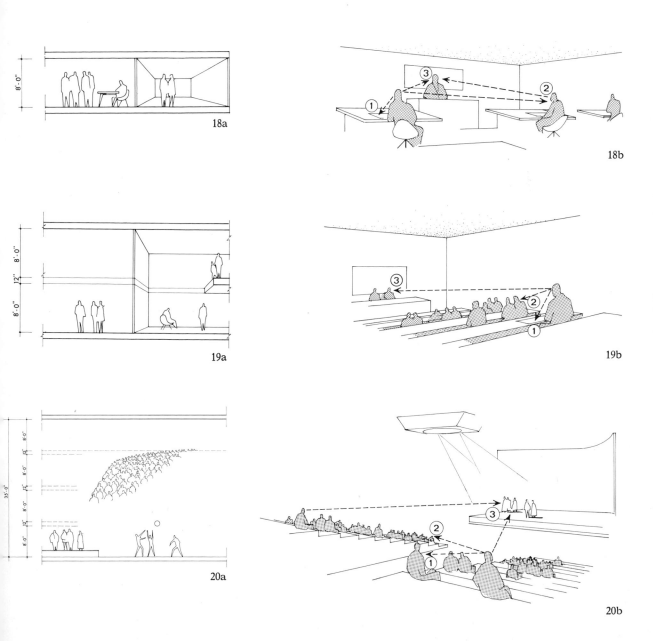

18a

18b

19a

19b

20a

20b

Industry, through technology, can supply the means to create Equipotential Space. It can supply both quantity and quality. The industrial procedure of designing and testing the new prototypes can bridge the gap between science, Equipotential Space, and available technology. The basic problem is how to transfer to the new methodology all the available talents not only from industry and professionals but also from society at large.

We need this combination of forces to start the new process. We must have a mass production of the Function Objects and Frame Components if we believe in an architecture for a mass culture. There is no doubt, in fact, that the only tested, guaranteed, totally accepted medium is the assembly line. This process is exact and fully proven; but before it starts producing, we need to clarify our input and our basic choices.

In mass production, we see the total use of metals, plastics, and other synthetics to the exclusion of natural materials. We no longer see leather upholstery and wooden parts used in standard automobiles, and the boat industry is switching from wood to plastic. Even the furniture industry is slowly abandoning wood, its classical medium. In fact, the trend toward excluding natural materials from the assembly line has been increasing in many parts of the world, and this trend is definitely totally irreversible.

Synthetic materials are all of predictable quality and are produced at a cost that can be estimated exactly.

Moreover, in mass production, structural safety factors can be substantially reduced in each of the elements in any component or subsystem, while dimensional tolerances at component interfaces can be held to manageable proportions.

For all these reasons—economy, quality control, weight, ease of transportation and fabrication—we will see only metals and synthetic materials used in the mass production of our architecture.

The present method of reconstructing cities cannot be carried on any longer. The substitution of parts in old buildings becomes prohibitive, due to the necessity of reproducing them by hand.

Our cities as they look today tend to disappear at a rate proportional to our economic growth and to the

VIII.
The Solution: Technical Means

Assembly-Line Processes for Mass Production Materials: Use of Synthetics · Self-Elimination of Today's City · Technical Appendix

Technical Appendix

With conventic
the following f

1. A *design*
hours) of not
for each build
2. The *desig*
the constructi
3. The *timii*
is unique to ea
and local labc
4. There is
transit and on
5. *Building*
slow to accep
proven superi
unsafe or ine:
codes.

In addition to
there are other
lowing:

1. *Purchase*
2. *Costs of*
public service:
3. *Costs of*
of social infra
centers, and s

In most case
30 per cent and
that reduction
to affect in a n
It is the total
be reduced.

Implied in a
financing neces
the piecemeal p
ently produces
small part of t
struction.

It is with thi
cuss a different
plore the imp
sources of dwe

United Natio
opment estima
housing constr
of Africa, Asia,
than 10 dwellir
people involved
per year. We se

increase in labor wages. Extensive urban areas in the major cities of the world have already disintegrated, and many others will follow the same path to extinction. But what is remarkable is the fact that even recent buildings are affected by the same decay, due to the difficulty of maintenance. They have been constructed mostly with obsolete materials and techniques. It now appears clear that a city must be built with mass-produced elements that can be rapidly substituted, while all the spaces must be kept efficient and able to house productive activities.

The interface between the industrially produced components and their physical settings—the building-to-ground interface—is the most expensive and most difficult problem to solve. One way of approaching it is to maximize the ratio between the volume of buildings and the number of unique ground interface conditions, using such concepts as megastructures. In this way it will be possible to place the same factory-produced building on any kind of land.

It is also important to decrease the time needed to construct a building. Life now is more rapid than construction time allows for. It takes almost as much time to build a house today as it did a century ago. A reduction in construction time would also mean a great saving on the total cost, because the cost of interim financing during the building stage is high and increases the need for early rental or sale.

Concerning the cycle of production, we must keep in mind that no less than three years will be needed between the design stage and the final marketing of the building.

By optimizing design and production time, the technological approach reduces the cost to society. Reduction in cost can shorten the necessary use-life of the house, avoid the formation of slums, and, in turn, create a more dynamic, flexible, and responsive market. In all societies, industrialized housing will begin to answer some of the problems raised by the dilemma of the standard—how to provide an equitable environment for everybody—through quality production at a predetermined cost.

In highly industrialized countries with a large consumer population, the production of housing by as-

sembly-line processes is already a real economical [...]
sibility. A new market for housing comparable to [...]
one that exists for the automotive industry has to [...]
created now.

At this point, the dilemma of the standard beco[...]
apparent in more precise terms. If advanced tech[...]
ogy is considered to be a device of highly industriali[...]
countries only, a line seems to be drawn between [...]
world's haves and have nots, and developing count[...]
would seem to be excluded. However, the necessit[...]
using advanced technology all over the world, e[...]
cially in developing areas, has already been pro[...]
Economic determinates are becoming less paroc[...]
for all countries, and unless autarchy takes over th[...]
areas, this could continue to hold true.

Clearly, experiences in the twenty-five years s[...]
World War II have indicated that in developing c[...]
tries the self-help system of housing construction [...]
the extensive use of unskilled labor has been ineffici[...]
time-consuming, and totally unsuccessful. Buil[...]
costs have been, in fact, much higher than corresp[...]
ing ones in industrialized countries. The reason is [...]
all necessary building equipment, from trucks to h[...]
saws and nails, has had to be imported, and at [...]
tremely high cost.

We are well aware that advanced technology pre[...]
poses an infrastructure of industrial organiza[...]
While mass need exists in every country of the w[...]
the necessary infrastructures must be establishe[...]
developing countries if an economical production [...]
be achieved.

As we begin to apply this technology, and as i[...]
turn, begins to permit us to come closer to an imm[...]
ate, meaningful response to our problems today,[...]
will find that Equipotential Space is an emerging [...]
ality.

Production of housing would have to follow all the typical phases of automobile construction: cutting and shaping of metal sheets; initial assembly of parts by bolting and welding; insertion of rigid parts and ducts for mechanical, electrical, and hydraulic systems (which also have bearing and stiffening functions); second assembly, injection of expanding plastics into predetermined areas; coating with plastic finishing materials; final testing and stockpiling.

Still using the automobile as an example, one can say that the appearance of structural metal parts that remain hidden from view can be rough, as long as ease in fabrication and assembly is assured. The objective is a sturdy product that can absorb variances incurred in the manufacturing process because the finish is applied in a very precise mold, thus guaranteeing the final shape and dimensions as designed. This method is contrary to the one prevailing in the construction of commercial curtain walls and other light metal structures in which the parts must be precisely built at every stage because most of them remain exposed. In fact, lightweight curtain walls can be examined as a typical example of a contemporary building product. At present, they are very expensive because of the labor involved in their manufacture and site-mounting. Because curtain walls act in one plane, the joints are extremely difficult to weatherproof, and the members display no unity of structural support. Moreover, because they are applied after the main bearing structure of the building is erected, they do not contribute to its static rigidity. This situation could be compared to modern automotive techniques which have evolved to the point where the body itself is the main bearing structure.

Past experiences with materials used by several industries for a technological application illustrate that the materials proposed in the approach discussed here allow one to consider the useful life of a building as very extended, if not indefinite.

Physical deterioration in existing buildings most often starts in the connecting points, especially where different materials meet. It will be necessary to carry out extensive studies to determine the combined behavior of metals and plastics with differing coefficients of expansion under long-term stress conditions. Very encouraging data is available from motor boats produced in the 1960's, which were up to 70 feet long and made from combinations of metal and fiber-glass reinforced plastics.

As far as maintenance is concerned, one cannot consider these materials, despite their extreme durability, to be infinitely stable, and the periodic replacement of joint-protecting materials has to be taken into account. A joint-system design must therefore incorporate a rapid and simple replacement method. In this regard, the future promises a wider use of stainless steel and other steel alloys, with a proportional cost reduction.

A brief glance at nonphysical obsolescence of an internal environment reveals that a longer use-life of a house can be guaranteed on the basis of the flexibility of functions and the consequent possibility of reshaping internal spaces.

Components of buildings will have to be designed to conform to regulations governing international transportation. In the future, the standard dimensions of these components will adapt to new developments in transportation technology. Transport on land can be by semitrailers, built for especially heavy loads, and drawn by tractors. These tractors can be equipped with devices to lift building components from the semitrailer, move them about the site, position them, and provide a platform from which final adjustments can be made (*Fig. 21*). When international regulations can be standardized, long-distance maritime transportation will be no problem, and normal stevedoring methods can be used to store building components both on decks and in the holds. Standard dimensions will also permit the use of helicopters in exceptional cases where other methods are not applicable (*Fig. 22*). Components can even be transferred from ship to shore by means of overhead cables, particularly if the building site is close to the waterway or no roads exist to the site (as in the case of islands) (*Fig. 23*).

The building site would be the final stage of the assembly line. Even laying the foundations would be a part of this process: Footings could arrive on the site ready for installation as hollow shells to be filled when in place. An assembly mold using lifting and coordinating devices could place components precisely in their designed positions. The final tool of the assembly line would be designed in coordination with the building components. Once in place, the components would be fixed and connected by parts within the system of jointing details.

The minimal allowance for tolerances in both horizontal and vertical joints must be continuously scrutinized and controlled so that in large projects errors would not multiply into serious discrepancies. Electronic control of these tolerances using photoelectric cells connected to a central panel equipped with warning devices has been already applied. This panel could

21–23. Handling of Components. 21. The drawing shows how a light, movable apparatus can assemble components and Function Objects. *22.* Components and Function Objects can be transported by truck or by helicopter. *23.* Components can be transferred from ship to shore by means of overhead cables when the building site is close to the waterway or when no roads exist to the site.

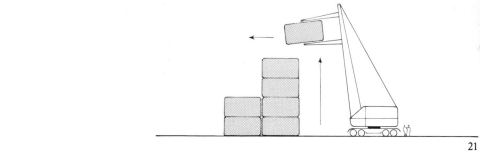

21

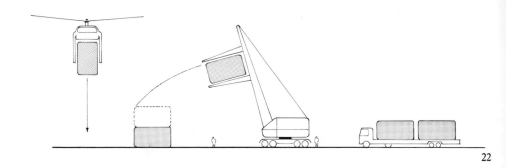

22

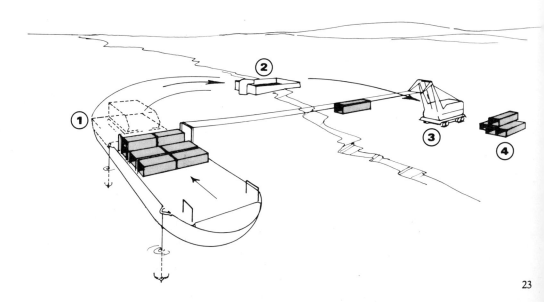

23

50

be connected to centralized computer installations, probably in the factory, which could oversee all phases of work on many sites. Orthogonal grids of cables could also be set up as guides for the positioning of components, with the individual cables themselves becoming part of the lifting mechanism. It is quite realistic to consider these operations in terms of a fully automated on-site assembly process.

Industrialization does not infer anything about the form of a design directly but has more to do with a methodology of organization and management. Its success is based on a proper conception of and a response to a problem in terms of performance and choice of materials.

In anticipating the results of applying the industrial process to the production of dwelling units, it is difficult to evaluate the actual cost of each unit without detailed knowledge of all its component parts. However, one can try to make an approximate evaluation by comparing the main components of the dwelling unit with several other industrial products. The results, if not entirely reliable for immediate use, will be indicative enough to justify some useful assumptions.

The price per pound is a basis on which the dwelling unit can be compared with other industrialized products. If one takes a representative set of the latter and determines the position of the dwelling unit among them, certain conclusions can be drawn. The price and weight of each of these products, complete and installed, can be found; from these, the cost per unit weight. The data are themselves quite variable, depending on many factors, but the following represent ranges of prices and weights derived from many typical examples in each category.

Electric boiler	$0.45—0.65/lb.
Washing machine	$0.45—0.70/lb.
Car	$0.70—0.85/lb.
Bulk carrier	$0.30—0.40/lb.
Passenger ship	$0.35—0.55/lb.
Tanker	$0.25—0.35/lb.

Cars and washing machines have many more moving parts than the proposed dwelling matrices (they incorporate greater concentrations of complex equipment), and withstand greater dynamic loads. They will, therefore, be more expensive to produce than the dwelling units. Tankers and bulk carriers also have to meet added problems of mobility and navigation, but their finishes are less refined than those of dwellings,

The passenger ship is probably most similar to high-rise, high-density dwelling units with fine interior finishes and extensive functional installations. However, the ship has mobility problems, and although it is made industrially, it is not mass-produced. These considerations would place the mass-produced dwelling unit somewhere between an expensive bulk carrier and an average passenger ship; that is, at about $0.40/lb. The unit price of $0.40/lb. is the cost of a highly industrialized product, fully finished, equipped, and installed.

The cost of $0.40/lb. presents the dwelling unit as an industrially produced product, but the figure is unfamiliar to architects, builders, and the average consumer. From previous exposure to costs of inhabitable structures, we find that all the data is presented as cost per square foot of floor area, or cost per cubic foot of enclosed volume. To facilitate direct comparison between the industrially produced dwelling unit and those of more conventional production methods, we must convert the cost per pound to a standardized data form: cost per area.

In 1966, a proposal for an industrially produced dwelling unit was submitted to the Common Market competition. This dwelling unit had a total area, including distribution, circulation, and communal areas, of 1,000 square feet.

A detailed study of one of this unit's basic elements, a floor panel, was made to ascertain information about the weight, strength, and cost of the proposed structure. In this study, two panels (S-1 and S-2) were under consideration. Both had large moments of inertia and were relatively light weight; S-1 weighed 8.5 lbs./sq.ft. and S-2 weighed 7.9 lbs./sq.ft.

On the basis of the results of this study, it was found that the industrially produced dwelling unit, including all finishes and services, would have a total weight of 20,000 pounds or an average weight of 20 lbs./sq. ft. With this information, the conversion is quite direct:

Total area of dwelling unit	1,000 sq. ft.
Total weight of dwelling unit	20,000 lbs.
Average weight	20 lbs./sq.ft.
Assumed total industrially produced cost	$0.40/lb.
or	$8.00/sq.ft.

These figures are particularly interesting for the United States, where there is both an enormous market and a high degree of industrialization. They should be compared with prices for other low-cost dwelling types; the normal low-cost high-rise unit using traditional construction methods costs not less than $15.00/sq. ft.

At present, finishes are of a rather poor quality. The semi-industrialized house with many small components, prefabricated in factories and site-assembled, costs $10.00 to $12.00/sq. ft. The figure does not include many essential fittings and finishes that must be applied at extra cost; nor does it include the furniture or the decoration.

Technical Details

The concepts and techniques used can be applied to any schematic prototype for any other panel-type components of the same scale and use.

It was decided that the finished floor panel (*Fig. 24*) should display the following characteristics:

1. Lightness (to facilitate assembly and transportation).
2. Minimal cost (related to an international market and scale of economics).
3. Resistance to variable range of loading conditions.
4. Jointing system designed to facilitate final assembly process.
5. Geometric configuration that facilitates ease of storage and transportation (stackability).

These aims have indicated two solutions: two types of panels of different internal structure. S-1 is based on a folded-plate structure, essentially a series of one-way beams that gain further rigidity from separate cross members. S-2 consists of pressed-steel truncated cones, welded in pairs to two flat sheets of steel, forming a space-frame structure. The two surface layers of polyvinylchloride (PVC), plus a filler, are then applied to the top and bottom. Insulated pipes and ducts are put in place before the top sheet of steel is welded on. The ratio of the moment of inertia to the unit weight of the panel is very large and signifies an efficient structure. However, in arriving at the correct weight-to-strength ratio, the weight must not be reduced to the point where extra labor would be required to produce the panels.

The cost of the panels is to be considered not only in terms of production and transportation but also in terms of any other process involved. Each operation in the production, delivery, and erection of a panel must be continuously checked and optimized in terms of time, labor, and cost of material and equipment. The precise optimization can be derived from intense studies based on experience.

The system of transporting, handling, and erecting

panels, as well as the system of connecting panels to panels and panels to vertical components relates to their lightness and manufacturing process. (Some designs for joints are illustrated in Fig. 24b.)

The technical aspects of the proposed industrially produced components (*Figs 24–36*) must be studied in terms of new approaches; these include:

Structure.
Protection of materials.
Fireproofing.
Galvanic current and lightning protection.
Weather.
Thermal insulation.
Acoustical insulation and sound absorption.
Electrical, mechanical, and hydraulic installations.

All elements can be considered as rigid structural entities, because they are built as three-dimensional frames and evenly distributed throughout the internal members. In case of multistory construction, extra steel reinforcing of welded plate or angle sections can be included in specific locations and can easily be augmented. It is also possible to allow a suspension cable to pass through cavities in the structure at certain points. Whole units can thus be suspended vertically from a bearing macrostructure. Being three-dimensional, the units provide rigidity as soon as they are secured. This is a distinct advantage over linear or single-plan members, which need bracing until the adjoining members are in place.

The problem of the foundations also has to be approached in a new way; constructing footings and connecting beams in reinforced concrete is very expensive and time-consuming, and in the case of a rapidly erected prefabricated building, it is not logical to spend a lot of time digging, forming, and pouring foundations. The prefabrication concept has to be carried through to the foundations themselves. Following the examples set by harbor engineers, caissons are a possible solution; in this instance they might be smaller, related to the loads they would support. They could be built in the factory, together with the other components, and be made of plastic-coated sheet steel or cast iron or even reinforced plastic.

If steel and cast iron were used, they could be placed on site as hollow shells and filled up with any material to add weight: sand, earth, and even water. Good results can be achieved by using protected steel forms filled with soil as foundations for very large and heavy engineering structures.

After the footings have been placed and filled, the connection to the superimposed structure could be effected by a telescoping device that rises from the footing itself and assures the absorption of any differences in site levels or discrepancies due to settling. Footings could also incorporate main pipe outlets and inspection openings; all the services at ground level would be incorporated within the foundations and pre-fabricated with them.

Protection from corrosion in a complex structure can be assured if one of these three measures are taken:

1. The entire structure of the panel is assembled first and a corrosion-resistant surface applied afterwards by immersion or electroplating.

2. The sheet metal to be used in the structure can arrive in coil form with a protective coating already applied. Welding can be by a high-speed process that does not damage the coating. Anodized aluminum can be included in this category.

3. The metal used in the structure can be a noncorrosive material like aluminum, stainless steel, or other alloys. A problem does occur at welded connections, where the material properties can change. There are also some difficulties if two metals in contact are far apart on the electrolytic table.

All the materials will have to be nonflammable. New international standards of fire-resistance ratings will be adhered to. The top of the floor component could be protected by the use of a layer of expanded asbestos. A coating of the same material could be used on the underside of the floor. These layers would serve not only as fire protection but also as a sound-absorbing material. Vertical members could also incorporate this material. The material itself could be composed of asbestos in conjunction with by-products of the oil-refining process. This combination has already been used in ocean liner construction and has proved economical, effective, and readily applicable. Spray applications of fire-resisting materials have been demonstrated as practical and are being accepted by more and more codes.

The inert plastic materials used throughout the structure in surfacing, joints, cores, and so on, can also serve as insulants against galvanic currents. Direct connections between different metals can be avoided by the use of plastic gaskets. No particular problems are anticipated in protection from lightning, present methods being adequate.

Plastic materials have already proved successful in protection against the elements. As far as dampness resulting from capillaries or water vapor is concerned, the proposed structures present no problems, because

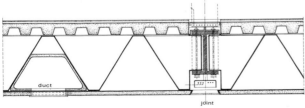

24. Floor Panel. Construction
made of thin steel plate (*a*),
and typical section (*b*).

25–26. *Floor Structure.* 25. Study and section of floor panel obtained with pressed-steel truncated cones, welded in pairs to two flat sheets forming a space-frame structure. 26. View and section of floor panel also illustrated in Figure 24. The structure is made of bent and welded steel plate. The top of the slab is made of a corrugated plate to be filled with a fireproof synthetic material for load distribution and soundproofing.

25

26

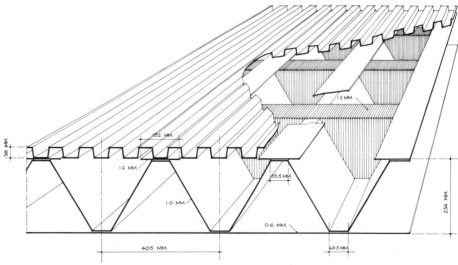

vertical members will be separated from the foundations at horizontal joints by impermeable materials, and the lowest floor will be separated from the ground by a ventilated space. The roof-covering consists of plasticized inert sheeting, applied to the roof panel in the factory so that an unbroken surface results. The joints will require the most careful attention, having replaceable neoprene gaskets sealed with adhesive tapes.

The expanded plastic materials proposed for the interior of panels will insure proper thermal insulation. Experience with this technique has shown that it can be used in large-scale production at very low cost. However, a problem arises at joints, where heat bridges must be avoided. It is, nonetheless, important to note that prefabrication methods demonstrate that metal finishes exposed to the sun transmit most of the heat, and not even very good insulation can properly arrest this transmission. Many experiments have shown that good insulation that reduces heat-bridge effects is possible through a proper combination of the materials and design.

In areas with a hot climate or with prolonged periods of sunshine, the proposed units will incorporate a *brise-soleil* system detached from the exterior wall and operated from within the unit. The angle of the blades will be altered to admit sufficient light but exclude direct sunlight. When a *brise-soleil* is separated from the external wall, an air current is induced up the face of the wall and overheating of the unit can be avoided. A double-roof system can utilize the same principle to encourage a flow of air between the two roofs, reducing the heat load.

It is important to note that what is in fact being suggested is that one design can be used in any climate; however, it must be flexible enough to allow for the differences these environmental conditions might present.

In order to insure adequate sound absorption, the acoustic insulation will be similar to that in an airplane whose 4-inch walls provide enough insulation to reduce the 130-decibel sound of a jet engine to an acceptable level. This is done with the use of fiber glass or similar absorptive material between layers of expanded foam-and-metal sheet. Further, the cabin interior is lined with highly absorptive material to help deaden the sound. The metal structure of the body is so connected as to reduce transmission by vibrations. Finally, all joints and seals are airtight and all openings are double-glazed with vacuum between.

The panels proposed can be even thicker than the walls of an airplane, but the construction principles

27. Air-Conditioning Schemes. 27a, b, c. Schemes of air-conditioning distribution obtained with ducts included in the floor panels. These panels are built to be assembled in many different ways to achieve flexibility in dwelling units. Shaded areas demonstrate possible solutions. *27d.* A valve is situated at the intersection of ducts.

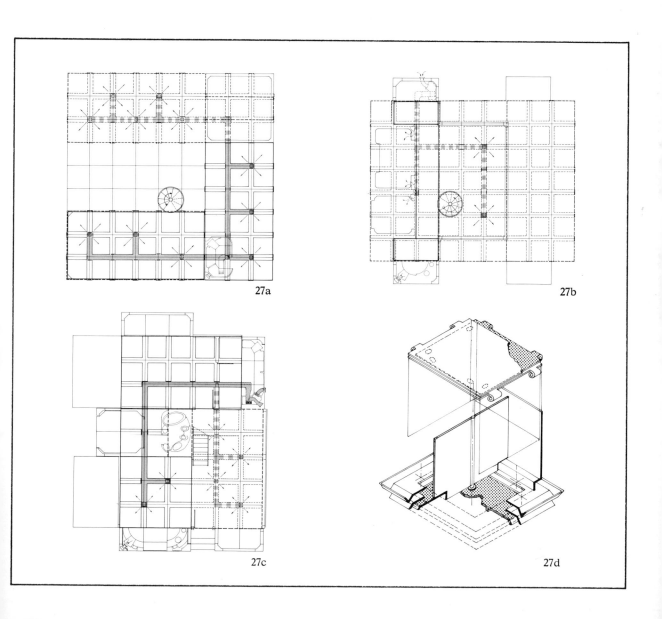

27a

27b

27c

27d

28–29. *Plumbing in Function Objects.* 28. Plumbing schemes in duplex dwelling unit where kitchen, bathrooms, and utility rooms are contained in the Function Objects attached to the façade. 29. The drawings illustrate the built-in plumbing and water distribution schemes in bathroom (*a, b*) and kitchen (*c, d*) Function Objects.

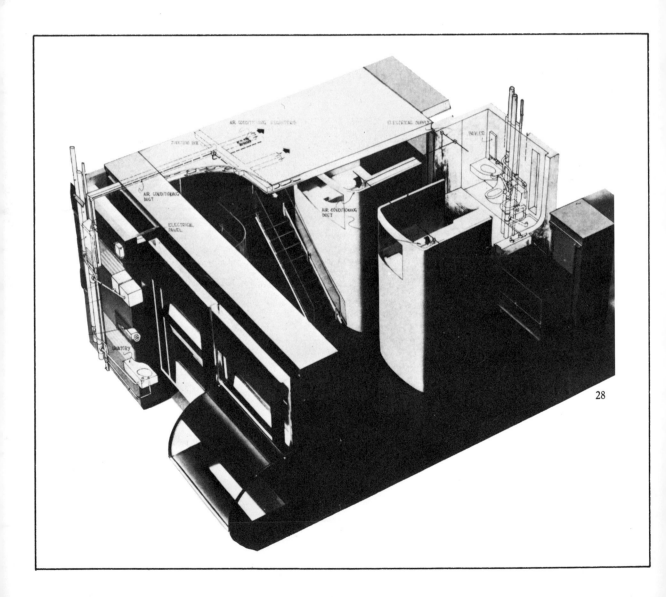

28

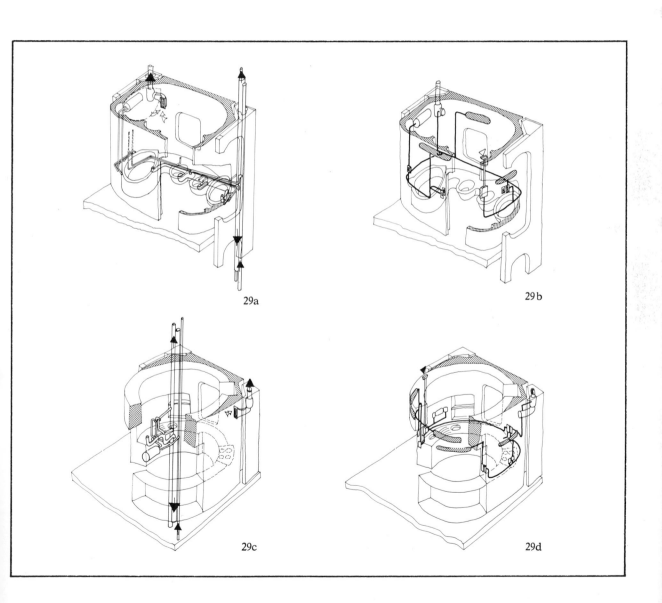

29a

29b

29c

29d

are similar. The panels will act as sandwiches of sound-absorptive material; the finishes on both interior and exterior will be sound-absorptive; the structure, being designed to reduce heat-bridge effects, will also reduce vibration transmission; the joints will have close tolerances and will be sealed to prevent passage of airborne sound.

The insulation for an industrialized building system is obtained not by heavy, dense walls but by light walls, with few but tight joints, and with sufficient sound-reducing materials throughout their depth. Expensive materials, such as fiber-glass matting, have to be efficiently placed in relation to required sound levels.

Mechanical, electrical, and hydraulic installations must serve flexible arrangements (*Figs. 28–29*). Their design must accommodate these stringent requisites and must also render their manufacture suitable to the assembly line. In fact, these installations are the primary elements to which the prefabrication concept must be applied. Therefore, they have to be studied as a series of standardized units, each as independent and self-sufficient as possible. It is important to avoid on-site junctions and attachments of many separate elements (electric wiring, hot-water pipes, and so on) in order to reduce assembling time and cost. These connections, like those of the automotive and aircraft industries, have to be made of durable, flexible materials. Even though their designs may be more sophisticated than rigid ones, they must be simple, cheap, and readily replaced, like a car's radiator hose. All the installations must have their predetermined places in the various structural elements and Function Objects. Inspection holes for all services will be in the joints between panels where all the service connections are located.

Each of the proposed dwellings will have an individual air-conditioning unit with ducts running throughout its wall and floor panels (*Figs. 27a–c*). The ducts will certainly be less expensive than in normal plants, being incorporated during the panel assembly. Typical previous air-conditioning systems included not only ducts suspended from a floor slab but a false ceiling to conceal them, duplicating the cost of the floor. Valves inserted into the duct junctions will allow selection of areas that are to receive air-supply. All panels will receive the same ducting during manufacture, but not all ducts will be required in all panels at the same time. Valves could then be used to regulate the flow of air within a given panel. The only on-site operations would be the linking of ducts by the flexible sleeves introduced above the adjustment of the valves (*Fig. 27d*).

IX.
The Solution: Proposals

Architecture of
Participation · Levels of
Choice · Flexibility
of Choice · Technical
Appendix

Industrialized construction is possible only through technology and systems, and Equipotential Space is possible only through industrialized construction.

These systems must include not only relationships among the actual physical construction units, known as hardware components, but also among all the production and decision-making processes, considered software, that determine the physical architectural environment.

That today systems are spoken of as hardware or software is symptomatic of the continuing dichotomy between art and science. Far from being mere engineering systems, architectural systems should include functional relationships between man's will and the control and direction of production processes. The physical design that results from the application of the system will be an expression of the available technology and of the aspirations of mass culture. Actual physical solutions will thus change constantly and be adaptable to cultural, social, and technological variety.

These relationships between will and ability—the dilemma of the standard and the actual choice of solutions—occur on several levels. These choices can be made by selecting from among predetermined components, combining and arranging these in any of the possible orders permitted by their forms. In any case, the general public must participate in choosing, thereby influencing the final design. Self-awareness, the level of education, and the level of self-government in the community will all combine to determine the actual mechanism of choice. It is not our aim to study or to understand how these choices are made; our task is to see how choices can be physically realized.

This process of assembling thousands of different environments using only a limited number of pieces is an involved and advanced notion. The inherent sociopolitical implications will concern many. Such a situation of almost instantaneous decision and result has no precedent in the history of architecture.

When we see that with a limited set of components the same kind of environment can be built on the earth as well as on the moon or Mars, we become aware that through the methodology of science, architecture achieves a new, universal dimension. These components will all be designed according to the same basic concepts of weight, transportability, and ease of assembly. Specific environmental conditions will be taken care of by a few special Function Objects.

In the context of our earthly existence, we are interested in the kinds of choices that can be made at five levels, into which we can divide the contemporary dwelling environment. Although purely schematic representations, these levels provide a helpful start for an analytical approach (*Figs. 30–31*).

1. The actual subsystem components chosen—the Function Objects and Frame Components.
2. Primary pattern level—the geometric organization of a single dwelling unit made of Frame Components and Function Objects.
3. Secondary pattern level—the small grouping of dwelling units: the neighborhood.
4. Tertiary pattern level—the geometric relationship between individual neighborhoods.
5. The city as a series of constantly changing and adapting patterns of neighborhoods.

Freedom of choice is wide at all five levels. We can say that the production of Function Objects and Frame Components belongs to the empirical sphere. At the same time, the choice of the form of the city or the reason for the aggregation of components can belong to the metaphysical sphere. This is to say that these two spheres can coexist.

In other words, the individual will be able to consider the Frame Components and Function Objects as purely industrial products of technology developed along market lines; at the same time, he can be sure that his decision will be respected concerning the mode of their aggregation. It will be possible for citizens to choose the quality and the mode of aggregation at all five levels (today, their freedom barely reaches to the second one). The relationships in Equipotential Space can permeate the entire urban domain and remain adaptable to change in the physical format, because the changes will fit the geometry of the pattern. If the pattern is finite or if spatial limitations are imposed, a static form will result, and the pattern will cease to be a living, growing, reacting thing.

Planners will become designers of multidimensional geometries rather than forms; of relationships between

30. *The Five Levels of Choice.*

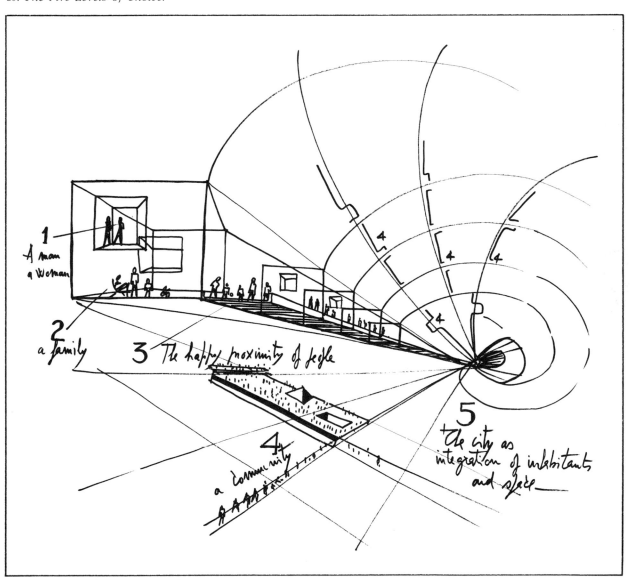

31. How Large Can a Community Be?

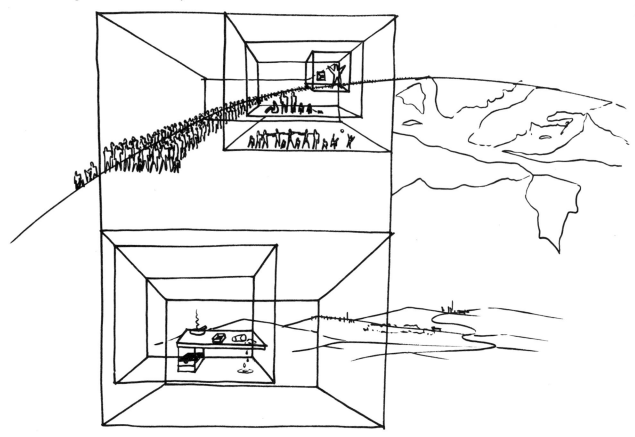

spaces rather than things. Through these relationships of patterns, we will achieve a new dimension of freedom, the capacity continuously to modulate any space.

One level of pattern is the individual dwelling unit, and here, also, Equipotential Space is meaningful. The space of the dwelling unit is not strictly continuous with the space of all the other levels of pattern, because today each family is considered a separate entity. However, as more and more areas are held in common, the pattern of the individual dwelling will become increasingly a part of the other levels of pattern, and the space will thus be continuous.

It is possible to take the situation as it is now, without changing anything, formulate a model in terms of today's needs, and design a system accordingly. Using today's technology, an acceptable dwelling unit with a capacity for interior modification or rearrangement can be constructed and marketed.

A realistic schedule for production and marketing of the results of present research and design would be five to ten years. With such changes in available technology as self-contained energy sources and life-support systems, our available options of life-style will change completely. It is on this basis that we can and, indeed, must start to apply the new methodology to our housing needs. That there will be future development is inherent in the system; we can only speculate where we will direct ourselves as we make our choices and take control of our future environment. As almost continuous personal mobility becomes a way of life on a global scale, and as technology allows us this independence, we may choose to live completely detached from fixed physical systems, wearing our houses on our backs or floating in balloons.

At any point in the process of decision-making, we will have the technical means of ascertaining the capital costs involved in any choice of components, patterns, or aggregations. If allowable cost per capita is known, a pattern can be determined to fit that total cost at a certain acceptable standard. The same standard at two allowable levels of cost per capita will result in two levels of space efficiencies and two sets of possible patterns. Even within these two pattern sets there are many possible solutions.

With this methodology comes the variety possible only through an industrial process. Using Frame Components and Function Objects to form patterns of solutions, we will overcome today's situation, in which apartment buildings look the same all over the world. One major difference will be in the primary pattern of the dwelling unit itself. As it becomes a more responsive, flexible, unique solution to specific situations, the occupant's need to decorate, which is compelling, in static and subdivided spaces, will disappear. Personal choice will be expressed instead in the spatial solution. Although the formal aspects of the Function Objects will be established by their industrial production, their combination in patterns will allow a great number of diverse solutions.

One possible solution would be to create an internal space as a continuous unified entity, space that does not need decoration but is itself a sculpture born of the relationships among Function Objects. The spatial unity of Renaissance houses may be translated into the volume of today's dwelling units.

Flexibility is a quality typical of Equipotential Space and is especially meaningful in the dwelling unit.

Our basic goal is to make this home as responsive as possible to the transformations the users devise. These transformations have two distinct objectives. One, of a physical order, is how best to use a small volume to serve all household activities; the other, of a psychological order, is how to modify the space to reflect a new equilibrium in reality.

It is naturally difficult to separate the two motivations by considering them of a totally different nature. In the first case, there is a motive that can be related to the division of the space among the members of the family. This has to be considered as more and more important because of the seasonal or even daily changes required by each member. Modifications in the volume can be carried out in several ways by different positioning of Function Objects or by replacing them with other models. When, for instance, the maximum free floor area is needed, all the Function Objects can be concentrated on one side of the volume.

Transformations of the psychological kind are less rational and deal with feelings and emotional reactions.

This personal dimension is the essence of the dimension of freedom. It is very subjective and involves the quality of the space in terms of light, volume, and tension.

The exercise of personal will in this sphere is one of the most important reasons for flexibility. The number of choices starts with the initial one concerning the Function Objects and goes on to subsequent ones concerning their arrangement. The freedom in this case can become almost unlimited as an appropriate and extended market is established.

Technical Appendix

In the recent past, housing authorities throughout Europe and the United States have been faced with the problem of providing low-cost dwellings for many millions of families. Studies by architects and engineers all over the world on ways to perfect standards for habitation have included some solutions already adopted. These studies have also searched for new systems of prefabrication that would reduce production costs; beginning in 1945, the history of European reconstruction is filled with illustrative episodes and (as always) is rife with lost opportunities. It was only after this period that the results of such experiences were carefully examined and a new approach taken, one of total industrialization in the construction of buildings. This assessment of previous action and this new approach were accompanied by a notable effort to clarify fundamental problems about the profession of architecture, the labor unions, and building codes. The search for new standards was the aim and common denominator for governmental agencies, industries,

32–37. Systems 1, 2, 3. Three schematic systems, which are fully described on pp. 85–122 and in Figures 32–126. *32, 34, 36.* These figures illustrate the basic Frame Components and Function Objects of the three systems. *33, 35, 37.* These figures show the basic bearing structure schemes and joints. The size of structural components increases progressively from System 1 to System 3.

SYSTEM 1

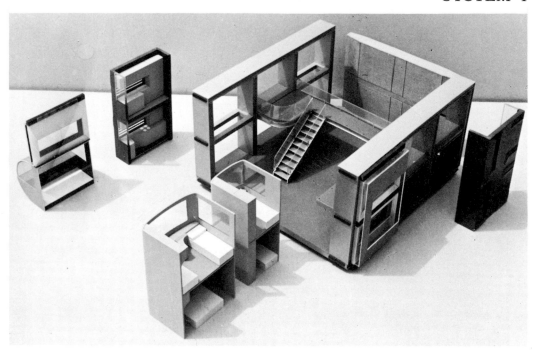

32

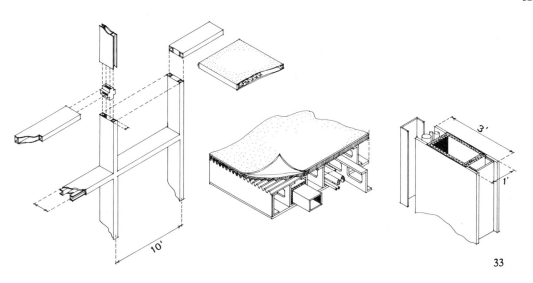

33

SYSTEM 2

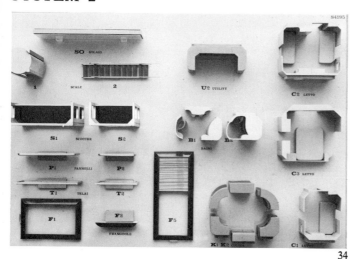

34

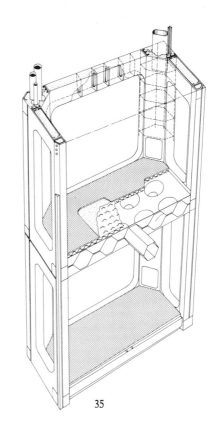

35

SYSTEM 3

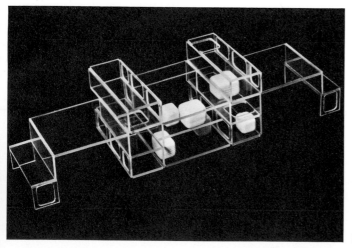

36

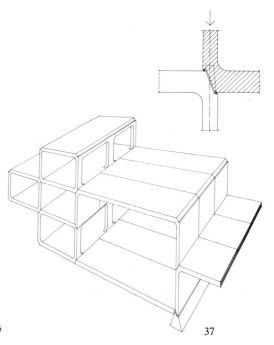

37

71

SYSTEMS 1, 2, 3

38. Systems 1, 2, 3. The three systems are used to build a dwelling-unit environment conceived as a continuous internal space (*a*), as opposed to the traditional apartment layout made up of a labyrinth of rooms (*b*).

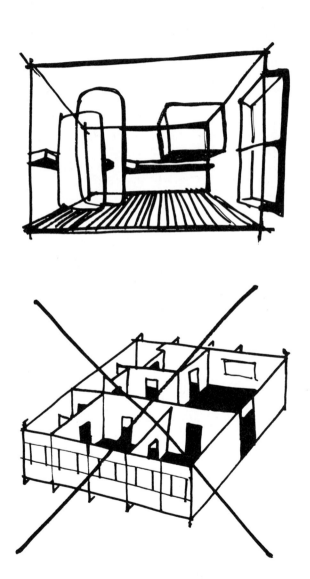

and even international organizations. In this regard, it was symptomatic when, in 1966, the European Coal and Steel Community sponsored an international competition for a totally prefabricated dwelling unit to be used both as a single-family house and in high-rise apartment buildings. The response included several hundred designs that arrived from the studios of architects, many of whom, judging from the quality of the material submitted, had already faced the problem and were able to offer valid new solutions.

The typical dwelling unit would house five persons, since it had already been demonstrated that the average northern European family was composed of parents, two children, and one other person. The same number is being adopted by many American standards, and most houses are produced with three bedrooms.

For these reasons, it seems logical to continue research by basing standards on five persons per dwelling unit and by considering the per capita space as between 200 and 240 square feet, exclusive of external corridors and centralized facilities (*Fig. 45*). Moreover, it has to be assumed that in the case of a duplex, the total area of each apartment would be calculated by adding together the plan areas of each 8-foot-high space. Thus, in the case of a unit of 24' x 24' in plan with a height of 17' (8' x 8' + 1') the total square footage to be considered would be 1,152 (576 sq. ft. x 2).

On the other hand, it is clear that world-wide requisites for housing do not concern only families of five persons. It seems certain, however, that it will be easy to obtain spaces adapted to a greater or a lesser number of persons living together when the systems are appropriately designed and therefore as flexible as required. Continuing research on a dwelling unit for five thus serves to focus the main objective on a typical problem of the times.

Flexibility: Flexibility will be the principal quality of future architecture, since it is the natural technological response to the pressures of modern life. Flexibility will be obtained by increasing the possibilities for the adaptation of any space to any circumstances whatever.

If one analyzes the processes that permit flexibility, it becomes clear that flexibility is a function of mobility and transportability and can be achieved mainly through a reduction in weight. If total industrialization is to be attained in the construction of buildings, light weight must be an inherent property of the finished product. It becomes apparent that the recreation of massive and heavy structures is by now completely senseless.

These analyses underscore flexibility as one of the fundamental achievements of modern technology, necessitating research that would distinguish and outline the limitations of a strictly technical response from those of an economic one. The second stage of this research would deal with the identification of precise relationships that exist between the degree of flexibility and the costs of construction and maintenance. Once this was known, it would be possible to establish the point at which it becomes economically feasible to mechanize the home to obtain almost total mobility of Function Objects, arriving at all the possible solutions within an extremely short period of time. The optimum possibility would be the one in which the desired solution is produced within a few seconds, by inserting in the programed control panel a coded release device. Obviously, however, the type of mobility most suited to each situation will have to be chosen according to whether the situation will be annual, seasonal, daily, or immediate. Acceptable solutions are the ones that make an effectively different use of space, not necessarily the ones (much greater in number) that are strictly geometric possibilities.

How to live in the best way possible and with the greatest freedom within a limited space? This question seems most important, especially if one considers that in the near future, hundreds of millions of new families will be living in spaces produced by industrial means. It will be necessary, therefore to initiate a study of prototypes that will allow for experimentation, particularly concerning the attractions offered by the interior environment. It will be necessary to establish all the possible uses of a small dwelling and ways to change the relationships of areas allotted to various functions and persons. After that, the occupants of a space will decide how to reshape it completely to their changing needs.

A duplex dwelling unit lends itself particularly well to interior rearrangement effected by the reallocation of Function Objects in various ways on either level, re sulting in a larger utilized area with less open space. The double height permits a true three-dimensional organization of the dwelling and a much larger number of solutions. Interior space thus reassumes the value that is lost in apartments constructed like small labyrinths. Moreover, the possibility of alternating double and single height permits a proper balance between utilized areas and free space.

There is the concrete possibility of producing a totally functional and psychologically satisfying environment within economic limits established by current markets in low-cost dwellings.

Interiors: A completely new concept of the mode of living will obviously have to assert itself as soon as possible, since it is inconceivable that housing for millions of new families will retain nineteenth-century standards. The overwhelming majority of dwellings constructed up to now (*Fig. 38b*) are nothing other than a series of small volumes formed by walls that must be decorated in order to avoid the sense of emptiness arising from a space without proper shape. Using furnishings for decoration is necessarily prominent and basic, since the walls of houses are now made deliberately for this purpose. This situation brings about the farce of stereotyped styles and decorative gimmicks.

The final result is that:

1. The cost of furnishing can approach the cost of construction. Even when the standard of furnishing is low, its cost is a substantial percentage of the construction cost.

2. The cost of maintenance and cleaning increases as solutions adopted become more elaborate.

3. Rarely are notable aesthetic results achieved with such interior spaces; at the same time, these solutions become obsolete very quickly.

For these reasons, it is evident that the low-cost dwelling unit demands new criteria for furnishing and decorating that will be economical but also capable of producing an appropriate liveability. A new dimension of the interior environment can be provided by Function Objects that would give to a large section of the public a choice of basic and efficient furnishings.

Many people will surely criticize such a proposal, citing the usual motives of the so-called personalization of every human belonging. Such people will not want to admit that the clichés of bad taste are fundamentally few in number and repeated throughout the world. To dispel the frustrations of those who are today forced to acquire cheap decor, at least a definition of new basic standards must be provided. To do this, we must study every function in the home and concentrate all the basic activities into fewer precisely designed spaces. This will occur only when a multiform and adaptable space within a low-cost dwelling can be obtained by adding to the living area volume saved through the use of Function Objects.

Thus, we are able to achieve a new kind of space in the small home (*Fig. 38a*). The designers and artists who no longer have any desire to apply themselves to the travesty of forms will have an opportunity to work with this new space.

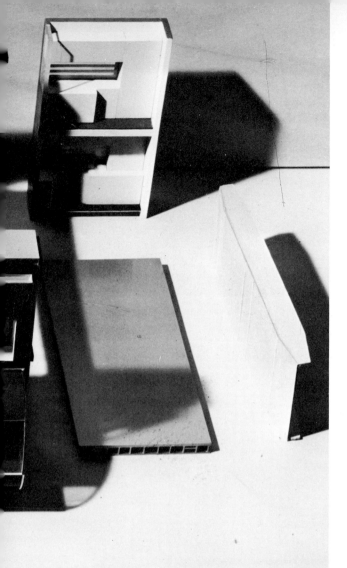

SYSTEM 1

39–40. System 1. 39. Frame Components and Function Objects. *40.* They can be assembled in various ways to form single-family units or multistory buildings.

39

40

41a

41–44. *System 1*. *41*. Typical bedrooms of System 1 that are always part of a two-story Function Object. *42*. A façade obtained with the assemblage of two Function Objects and a window panel. *43*. Typical bathroom (*a*), and kitchen and utility room (*b*) Function Objects. *44*. A possible layout of the dwelling unit. Left: Plan of the upper floor. Right: Plan of the ground floor.

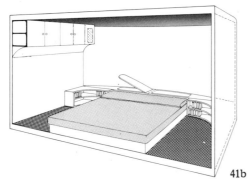

41b

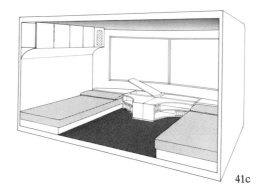

41c

42

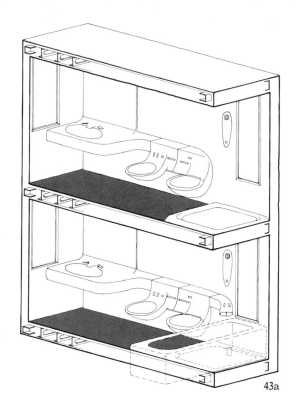

43a

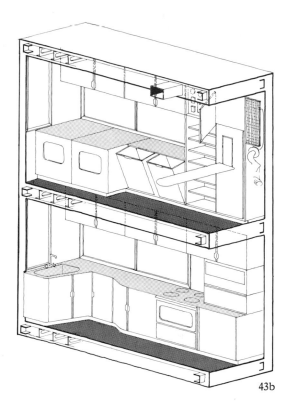

43b

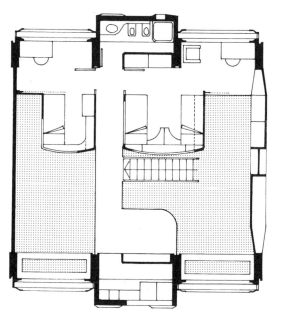

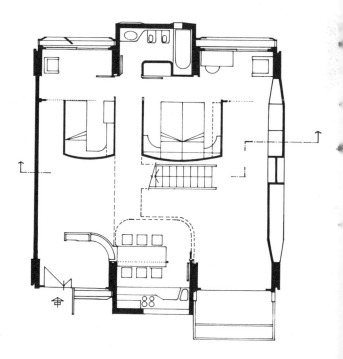

44

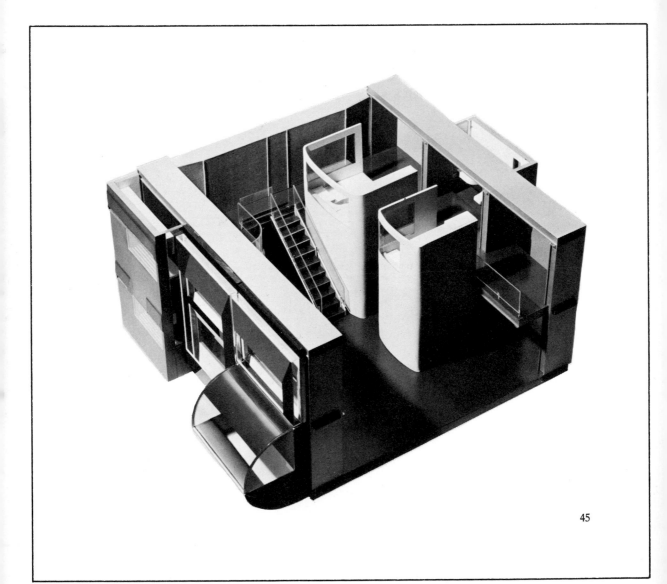

45

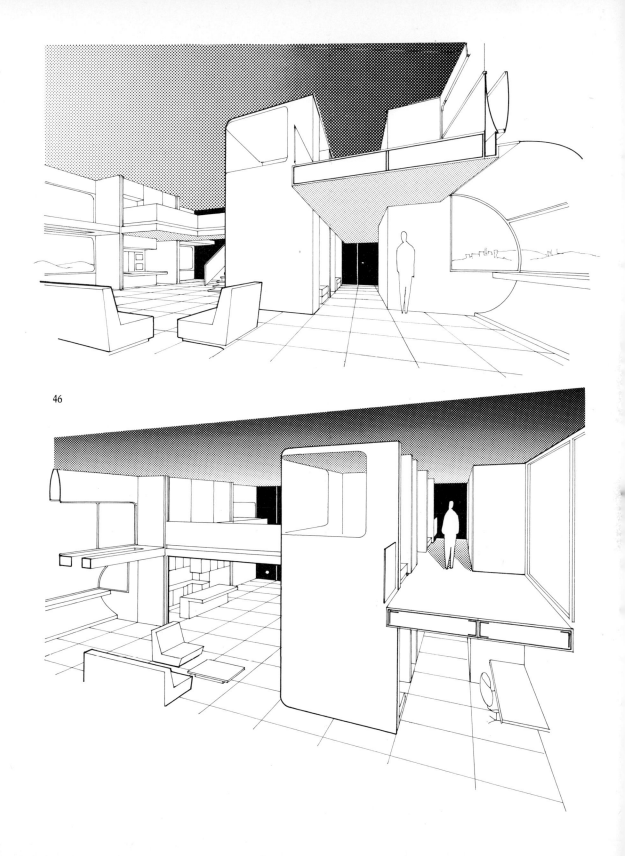

46

47–48. System 1. Two possible solutions for dwellings obtained with System 1. Kitchen, bathroom, and utility rooms can be placed in various ways on the façades, while bedroom Function Objects can be moved in the internal space. Figure 48 shows a dwelling that has one module fewer on the ground floor (*b*).

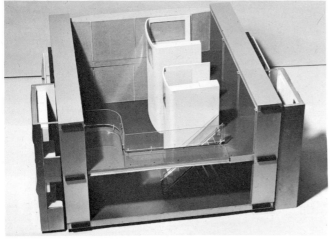

47a

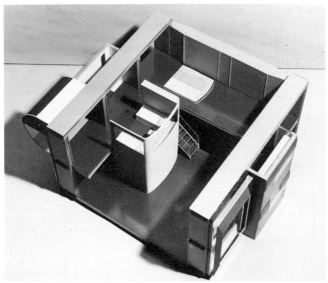

48a

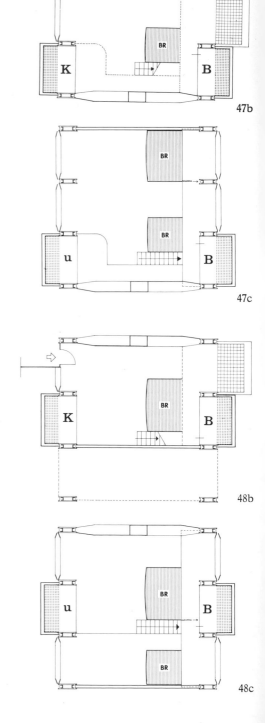

47b

47c

48b

48c

Aggregation of Components: The designer will have to identify all the possibilities of aggregation of the components in order to utilize their capacities.

In formulating criteria for planning a system, it becomes apparent that there are four types of variables:

1. The geometry, which allows for the interchangeability of components.

2. The technology to be employed.

3. The interior volume resulting from the possible combinations.

4. The aggregational capacities at an urban scale and the adaptability to topography for the possible types of macrosolution.

Function Objects play no part in the study at this stage, since they could have already been designed and would thus be considered as established constants.

Regarding the first variable, geometry, a number of components must be found that would permit several unique aggregations. However, for reasons of production and utilization, it would have to be as limited a number as possible (*Figs. 32–37*).

For the second variable, the technology employed must permit a great variety of solutions without adding to the total cost due to excessive adaptability and sophistication.

It is obvious that the result of research on the third variable would be both an interior and an exterior space, each with great potential as an adaptable environment. Many systems are certainly extremely adaptable as far as the number of solutions for aggregation is concerned.

Relative to the fourth variable, it is necessary to specify that basic patterns are of three types: (a) horizontal pattern; (b) inclined or terraced pattern; (c) vertical pattern.

Type (a) could rest on the ground or be detached from it by means of a bearing macrostructure. The former would allow the inhabitants to live on the ground, with garages nearby, and would permit total exposure to sun and sky; it has all the qualifications of the age-old Mediterranean house and also the capacity to provide the privacy and efficiency featured in contemporary dwellings. Moreover, because there are no vertical links, it allows for a successful communal life, although there are limitations to the possible views from the dwelling units. It is foreseeable that a high density of construction of this type, with emphasis on its very low costs, would generate an enthusiastic acceptance by the public (*Figs. 67–71*).

Type (b) could also rest directly on hilly terrain. In this case, it would be necessary to design a pattern capable of adapting to any ground, so that the same components could be combined in different ways without changes in the module (*Figs. 114–17*). Erecting the same building on level terrain would produce spaces under the terraced part that would be almost triangular and would tend to decrease in width from the base upward. These spaces could be used as garages or for centralized communal facilities. It is obvious that in considering the width of an apartment plus the exterior terrace (about thirty feet) the area that remains between the sloping line and the vertical line would increase proportionally with the increase in height of the entire structure. In order to determine the appropriate height, the relationship between the area of the apartment and the residual internal spaces would have to be resolved so that the latter area would not remain unutilized on the lower floors.

This type of construction could also be very inexpensive, especially when it redeemed very steep and otherwise unusable terrain. Furthermore, as can be readily understood, type (b) affords many possible advantages, such as privacy and views of the land and sky.

Type (c), as it rests on the ground, has long been the best known and most commonly assumed high-density solution (*Figs. 40 and 49*). But it is not so common when the prefabricated components are supported by macrostructures (*Fig. 51*). This technique is already in use and affords rapidity of assembly as well as clearance from the ground, especially if used in extended developments.

The macrostructure could also be prefabricated according to a system that would consider (for the horizontal framework as well as for the vertical) various solutions using the same components. Likewise, it would be possible to improve vertical or horizontal transportation means by attaching them to the same structure.

Two factors would enable buildings, including large and complete structures, to be moved from one site to another: lightness of the components and transportability of Function Objects. Moreover, in the case of a very mobile family that uses two or more dwellings in different localities, it would be possible to transport just one set of Function Objects from one place to another.

The Function Objects for five persons would fit onto a truck fifty feet long and could contain all clothes, household utensils, and other domestic necessities, including small furniture from the living areas, which would be stored within the Function Objects during transportation.

System 1: This was the initial formulation of a dwelling structure configuration (*Figs. 39–49*). The bearing elements, both vertical and horizontal, are panels of various sizes and thicknesses, connected at joints by bolted links. The spaces created by this load-bearing frame would contain two types of elements:

a. Function Objects (bathrooms, kitchens, utility rooms, and so on). These will be attached to the frame externally in many arrangements and connected to the main pipes and ducts contained within the structural frame.

b. Infill panels (doors, windows, cupboard panels, and so on) of System 1 would be typical structural elements (columns, beams, and slabs), but would be lightweight factory products with built-in mechanical, electrical, and hydraulic systems. The basic element is a sandwich panel made from sheet steel of various thicknesses, stamped and assembled, complete with pipes, ducts, insulations, and plastic coating. The advantages of this system are that it is made of relatively small parts, insuring easy transportation, and that it is capable of becoming an open system to which many products and designers can contribute. However, the main disadvantages are the large number of on-site operations in connecting joints and the problems of rigidity and weatherproofing. Thus, many of the imperfections of existing heavyweight systems of prefabrication are retained.

System 2: This represents a subsequent development (*Figs. 50–71*). The vertical structural components are conceived as rigid three-dimensional entities. They are made to a fixed height but their width is equal to two or three times the basic module (4 feet). The structural system is completed with the inclusion of modular floor panels.

Function Objects can be placed in various ways in the internal space, attached to the vertical elements, which again include pipes and ducts. Another group of components is used as infill panels in a similar way to those of System 1.

The manufacture of structural elements is also similar to that of System 1: Sheet steel is stamped, welded, and completed as before. The structural rigidity of vertical elements achieved in the factory is an improvement over the previous machine, but the fact that vertical and horizontal elements are still two distinct entities raises many problems of on-site stiffening and jointing. However, the number of pieces—and consequently the number of factory operations—is a reduction from the previous system.

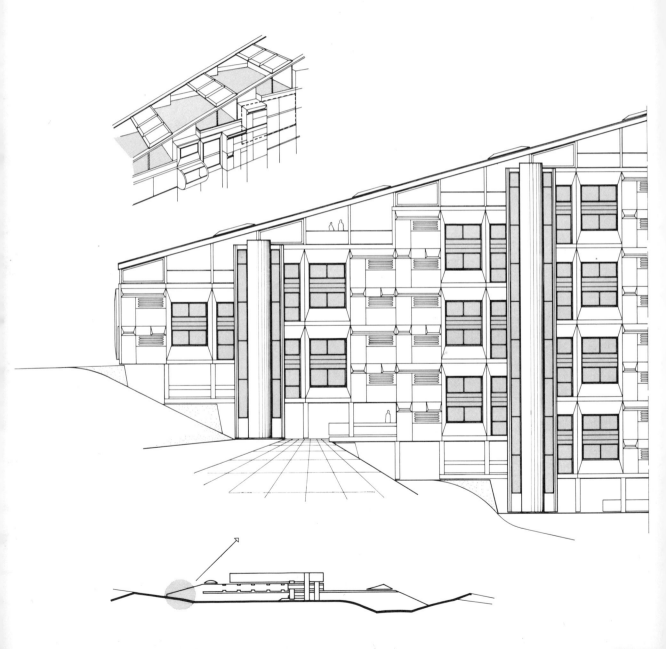

49. *System 1.* Studies of macro-aggregation of dwelling units (see Figure 40). Dwelling units of different sizes can be assembled in various ways to obtain several façade designs.

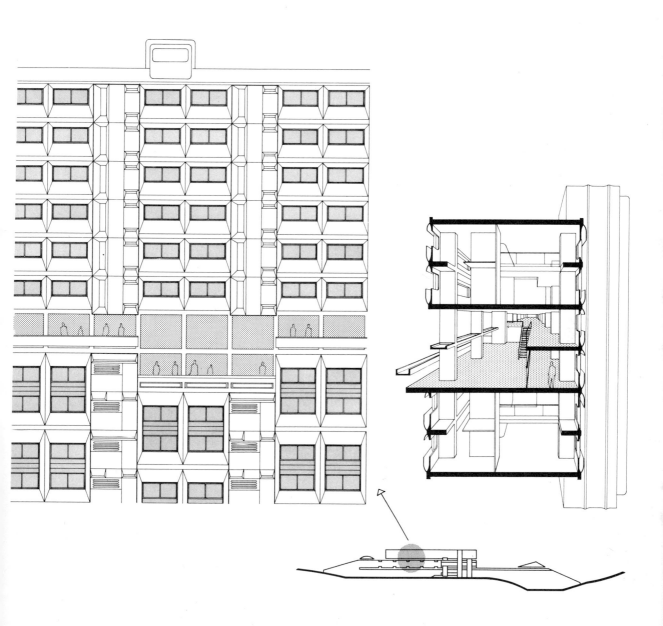

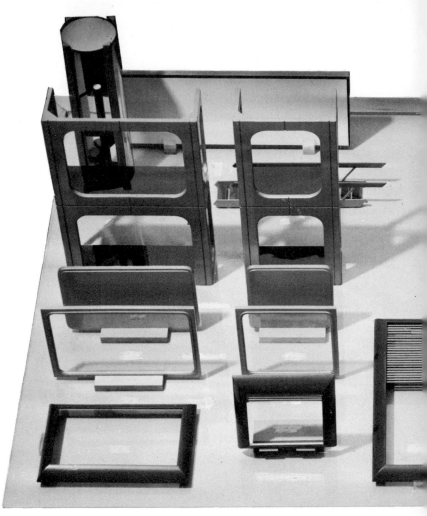

SYSTEM 2

50–52. *System 2. 50.* Frame Components and Function Objects. On the left side, the structural components and external panels; on the right side, the Function Objects. *51.* Components can be assembled in various ways and, as is described in this model, can be hung by cables from a macrostructure. *52.* This describes a section of the structural system shown in Figure 51. Due to the light weight of the system's components, similar assembly can be economically obtained when it is necessary to preserve the continuity of a landscape.

50

51

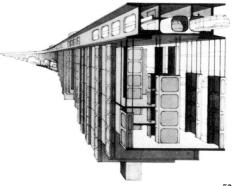

52

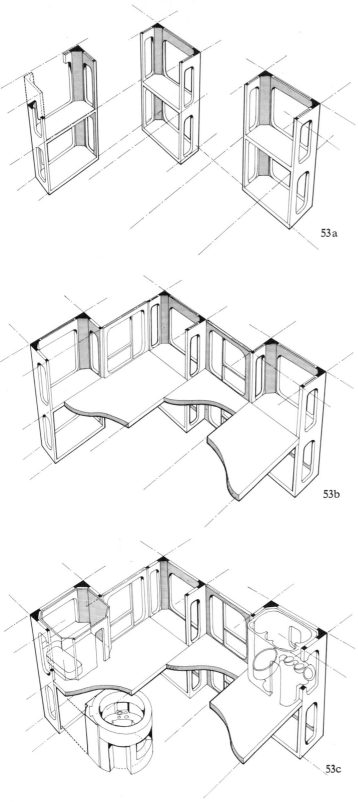

53. *System 2.* The assembly of the system's Frame Components and Function Objects. In phase 1 (*a*), vertical components are placed. In phase 2 (*b*) floor-slab and window panels are connected to the vertical structure. In phase 3 (*c*) Function Objects are placed and connected to the main pipes and ducts. The positioning of Function Objects can be easily changed after the building has been erected.

53a

53b

53c

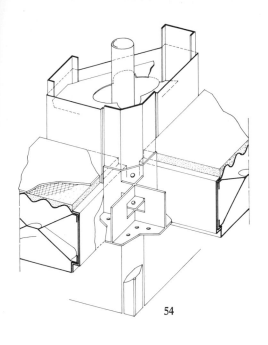

54

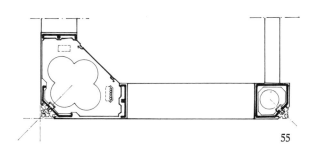

55

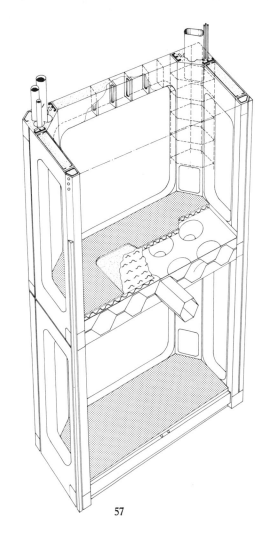

57

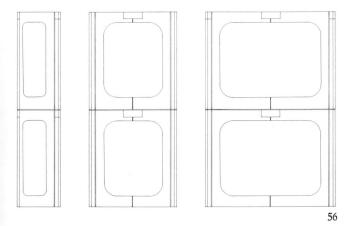

56

54–57. *System 2.* Structural and mechanical details. *54.* Joint of floor panel to vertical bearing structure. *55.* Detail of tridimensional vertical structure that shows in plan the corner where the vertical pipes are located. *56.* Elevations of tridimensional vertical structures that will contain Function Objects. *57.* Isometric of tridimensional vertical structure showing the connections of the air-conditioning ducts.

58–60. *System 2.* Function Objects. They have neither ceiling nor floor, because they are to be inserted in the tridimensional vertical structure, which also provides the utility connections. *58.* Bedrooms. *59.* Kitchens (*a*) and plans of kitchens (*b*). *60.* Bathrooms (*a*) and plans of bathrooms (*b*).

58

59a

59b

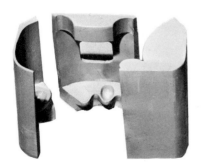

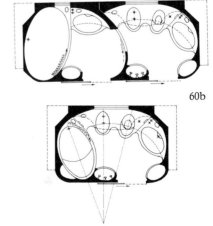

60a

60b

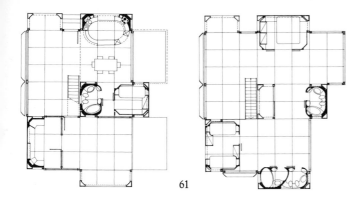

61–62. *Dwelling-Unit Type 2A. 61.* Left: Plan of the ground floor. Right: Plan of the upper floor. Many dwelling layouts can be obtained by exchanging positions of Function Objects. *62.* Architectural view.

61

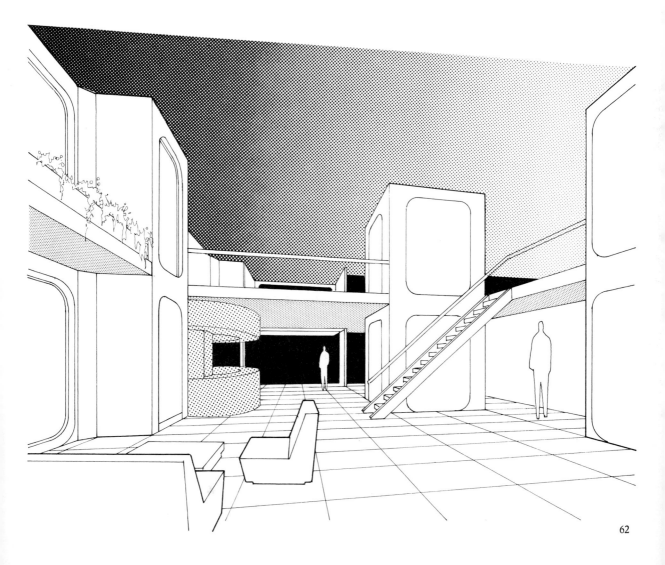

62

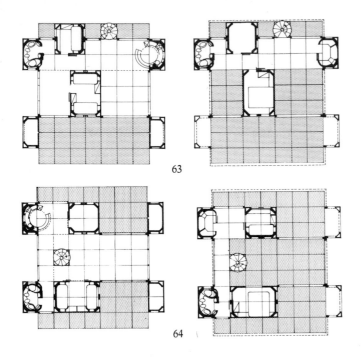

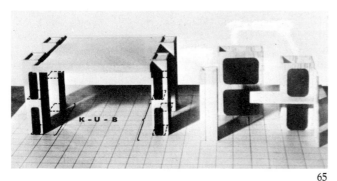

63

64

63–66. Dwelling-Unit Type 2B. 63, 64. Plans of dwelling-unit type 2B that are conceived as single-family houses. Left: Plans of lower floors. Right: Plans of upper floors. *65.* Scheme of the flexibility of the dwelling. Bedrooms (right) can be positioned in many ways under the roof (left). *66.* Perspective showing various possibilities of aggregation of dwelling-unit type 2B.

65

66

System 3: This (*Figs. 72–117*) is a logical development of the previous two. The components are three-dimensional in form and structure. Structure and construction are effected with only a few major elements, and assembly is simpler than with the previous examples. Within the structural pattern, Function Objects, complete in themselves, are free to be moved to any position in single- or double-height volumes (8 feet or 17 feet). At joints, the elements overlap and are linked by rigid connections. On-site operations will be minimized, and each dwelling unit will be made of a few superimposed components that will arrive completely finished from the factory, two or three truckloads per dwelling unit. Despite the limited number of components, there are many possibilities of unit combination and configuration.

The principles of the concept of System 3 are applicable even if different materials are used, as long as lightness and factory-process-suitability are retained.

A Dwelling Unit Model: A full-scale mock-up of System 3 was constructed in the engineering laboratory at Columbia University in the spring of 1968 by students of the School of Architecture (*Figs. 98–111*).

The model, with a base of 24′ x 24′ and a height of 17′, was built of polystyrene and wood, using mechanical laboratory equipment, including a traveling gantry and a crane, to move the Function Objects and the intermediate floor into various positions. The assembly consisted of a rapid system of cutting polystyrene tubes of 12″ diameter and 1″ thickness into four parts and joining them to each other to form rigid structures; into these were inserted polystyrene panels of 1″ and ½″ thickness (*Figs. 101–4*). Wood was used for the intermediate floor and the staircase as well as for the rudimentary cantilevered arms, to allow flexibility in the movement of Function Objects. The model was not conceived as a design for a dwelling unit but simply as a machine for studying spaces. For this reason, the six Function Objects and the intermediate floor were rearranged and displaced repeatedly in all the possible positions, creating many configurations of the volume. Thus, the variations offered by these solutions, as well as the simplest type of mobility that would allow this flexibility, were studied. Special attention was devoted to the analysis of spaces resulting from the different arrangements of the Function Objects. From these observations, the following results emerge:

1. The total space, consisting of eighteen unit volumes each measuring 8′ x 8′ x 8′, plus six Function Objects

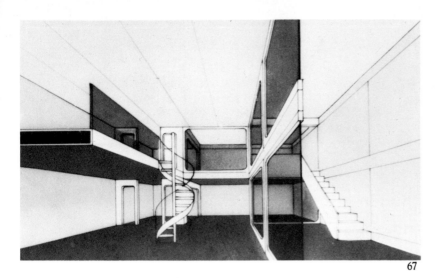

67

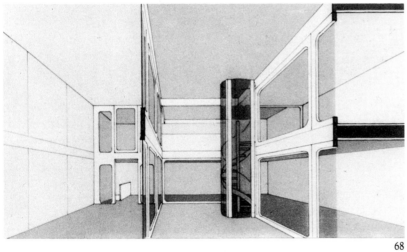

68

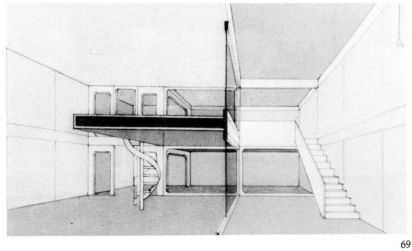

69

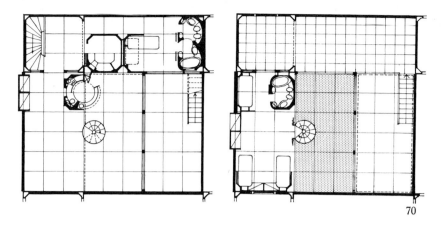

67–71. Dwelling-Unit Type 2C. 67–69. Three different spatial solutions that can be obtained with dwelling-unit type 2C. 70. Plans of dwelling-unit type 2C. 71. Model of typical aggregation of type 2C, showing the main bearing structure and the internal panels, which can be rearranged to form different solutions. Unit receives natural light from internal courts.

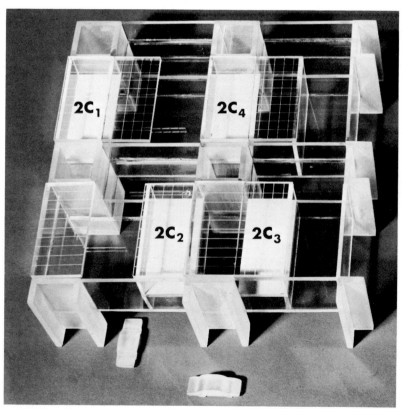

placed within (their total volume being equal to five unit volumes), proved extremely adaptable. The various acceptable solutions can number in the hundreds.

2. Extremely diverse configurations of spaces can be produced, as if each had been generated from a different mold.

3. It is possible to obtain ample free spaces by concentrating all Function Objects in one part of the dwelling. Considering that the total area was 1,152 square feet (24' x 24' x 2'), it must be noted that it is impossible to obtain similar results in conventional dwelling units of the same area.

4. A high degree of flexibility makes a small dwelling unit capable of total modification, and it can offer a large space for every different situation. Thus, for example:

a. If a lot of space is desired for children's play activities, it would be possible to locate their bedroom and one bathroom in such a way as to allot the necessary area to them.

b. If a large free area is desired on the lower floor, the Function Objects can be concentrated on the upper floor.

c. When strong illumination and a spacious free volume are desired, the majority of the Function Objects could be concentrated on the side of the dwelling opposite the windows.

5. The compact volume of the dwelling is what contributes most to maximum flexibility, and it is also economical, having only one exposure.

6. In the case of the prototype, the volume and the area of each Function Object, even if they are not the minimum possible, can be considered as very contained. The master bedroom is 11'8" x 8', and the other two bedrooms 8' x 8'. The kitchen is 8' x 5'6" (*Fig. 102*). It may be observed that a slight increase in the above areas would lead to a notable increase in free interior space within the Function Objects, while the ratio between free volume and the volume occupied by them would be barely affected.

On the basis of these considerations, two fundamental problems emerge clearly:

First, there must be an economic study of flexibility to determine mobility-time and mobility-cost relationships. In this regard, it will be necessary to discover whether the mechanism best suited to move and lift Function Objects is an apparatus that could move freely within dwellings or whether it should be incorporated into the fixed structure. Moreover, we must consider that, in order to increase flexibility, Function Objects could be dismantled and their parts reassembled in various combinations.

Second, there must be optimization of the relationship between total volume and the volume of Function

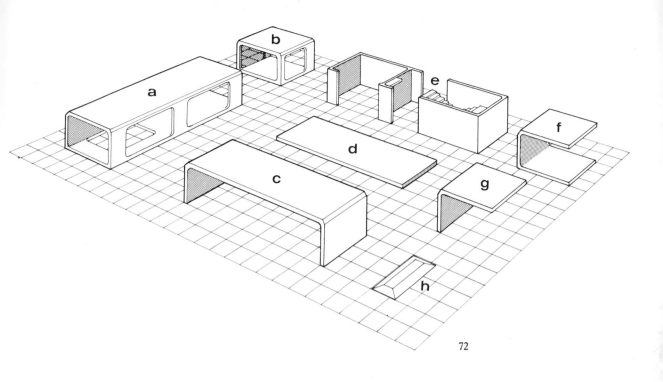

72

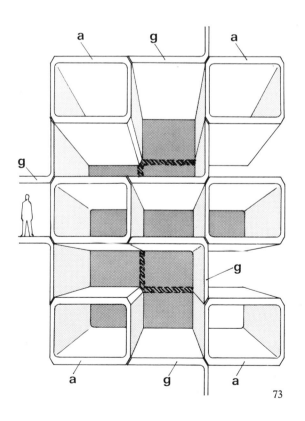

73

SYSTEM 3

72–73. *System 3.* Frame Components. Figure 73 shows a possible aggregation of components forming dwelling units of different shapes and sizes.

Objects. In this process, possible solutions would take into account many factors concerning not only the inch-by-inch gauging of all the interior parts of the Function Objects but also the relations of the latter to regulations governing transportation. Once this is accomplished, it will be necessary to proceed to a new measuring and comprehensive reassessment of all the interior layouts of the dwelling unit.

The full-scale model, as a machine, has therefore responded very well to the test and has demonstrated that the prototype is the most valid means for analyzing an interior space.

LEGEND

Symbols for Systems 1, 2, and 3:

Function Objects	Bathroom & Toilet	B
	Kitchen	K
	Bedroom	BR
	Utility and Mechanical Room	U
Frame Components	Three-Dimensional Components	a, b, c, d, e, f, g, h, and so on.

Type of Dwelling Unit

System 1	Solutions obtained with different positions of Function Objects: 1A1, 1A2, 1A3, and so on.
System 2	Solutions obtained with different positions of Function Objects: 2A1, 2A2, 2A3, and so on.
	Solutions obtained with different positions of Function Objects and of Frame Components (vertical structure and roof do not move): 2B1, 2B2, 2B3, and so on.
	Solutions obtained with different positions of Function Objects and Frame Components (including roof but excluding vertical components): 2C1, 2C2, 2C3, and so on.

System 3   Different aggregation obtained with the use of three-dimensional components: 3A, 3B, 3C, 3D, and so on.

Solutions obtained by different internal layout of Function Objects and movable floor: 3A1, 3A2, 3A3, and so on. 3B1, 3B2, 3B3, and so on. 3C1, 3C2, 3C3, and so on.

Following the experiments on the full-scale mock-up of System 3, a new model (*Figs. 118–25*) was developed and studied. Spatially, it is an extension of System 3; however, it differs in that it has both structural Frame Components and mechanical Frame Components.

One mechanical Frame Component comes with the Function Objects and includes the window. It is assembled in the dwelling-unit volume and, except for connections to basic utility services (sewer, gas, electricity, and so on) at one corner of the unit, it is structurally and mechanically autonomous. The circulation passages (including the one within the window frame) contain all the pipes and ducts.

In this way, a total freedom can be achieved in the volume, because all geometric choices become possible The spatial volume is part of the pattern and can be modulated with sophisticated moving equipment. Only the connections to the corridors or to the vertical elements will need mechanical connections.

Because of this, it will be easier to move all the Function Objects to other volumes without expensive equipment.

The dwelling unit can even reshape itself according to a number of preprogramed patterns. This reshaping cycle can be reprogramed every day (for instance, on a two- or three-hour cycle). In this way, a very small volume can be totally exploited to serve all the necessary dwelling-unit functions in an optimum way. Although this may be an extreme solution, the cost of the flexibility could be less than the cost of the volume saved in a dense urban situation.

The Function Objects are moved vertically by a lifting device incorporated in the window unit (part of the mechanical Frame Component) and a carrier that moves horizontally through the space. There are two vertical positions and nine horizontal ones, so all eighteen unit cubes in the dwelling-unit space can be reached. All movement must be orthogonal and only along one component axis at a time.

In addition to the Function Objects, floor panels are provided to augment the second-floor-level area.

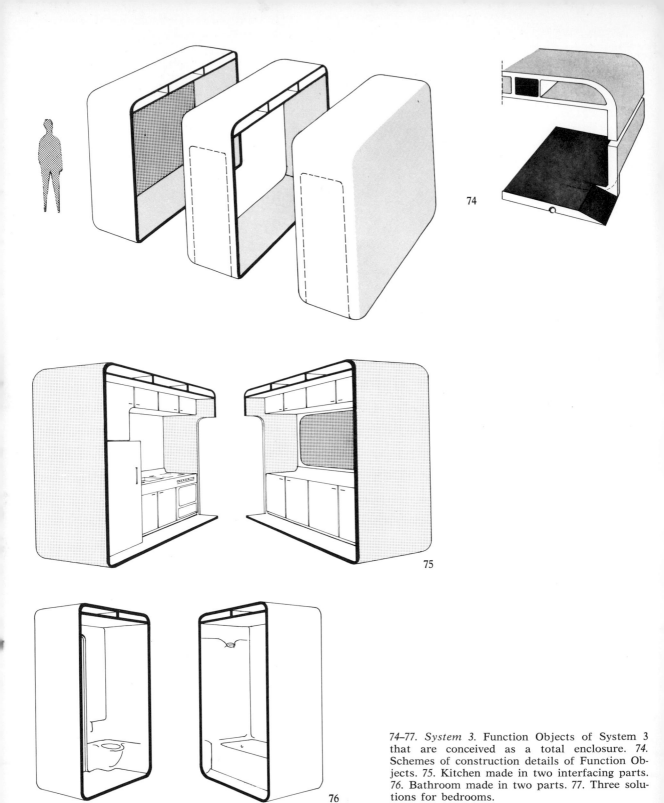

74–77. *System 3*. Function Objects of System 3 that are conceived as a total enclosure. *74*. Schemes of construction details of Function Objects. *75*. Kitchen made in two interfacing parts. *76*. Bathroom made in two parts. *77*. Three solutions for bedrooms.

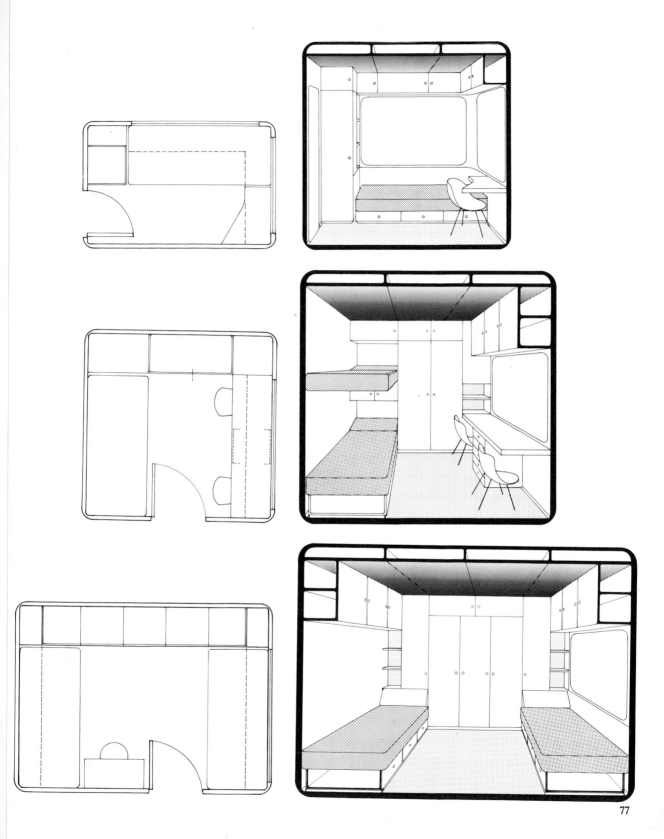

77

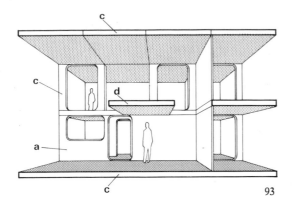

93

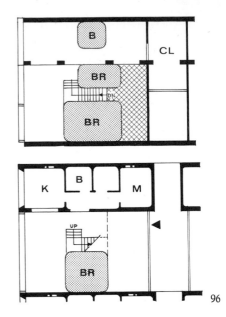

96

93–97. *System* 3. Solution for dwelling unit 3D obtained by the aggregation of Frame Components types (a, c, d). 93. Longitudinal section—perspective of the dwelling. 94. Bathrooms and kitchen are contained in the Frame Component type (a). 95. Interior perspective of the dwelling. 96. Dwelling unit layout 3D1. Above: Plan of the upper floor. Below: Plan of the lower floor. 97. Dwelling unit layout 3D2. Above: Plan of the upper floor. Below: Plan of the lower floor.

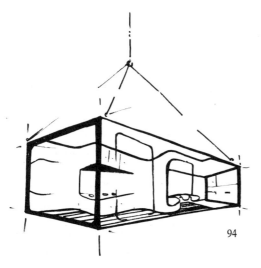

94

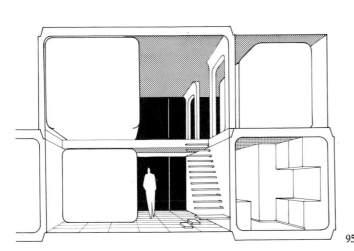

95

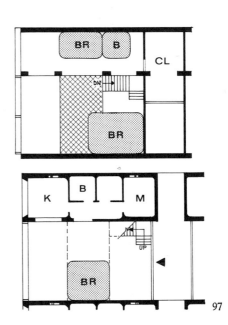

97

98. *Full-scale Mock-up of Solution for Dwelling Unit 3E*. Built by students of architecture at Columbia University, New York, in the engineering lab. Internal perspective taken with fish-eye lens.

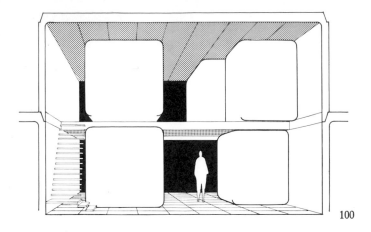

99–102. *Columbia University Full-Scale Mock-Up.*
99. External view of the mock-up. Function Objects were moved inside the structural envelope to test internal spaces. *100.* Interior perspective of the dwelling. *101, 102.* Internal views of layout. The shapes of Function Objects and other internal components are only schematic.

100

101

102

111

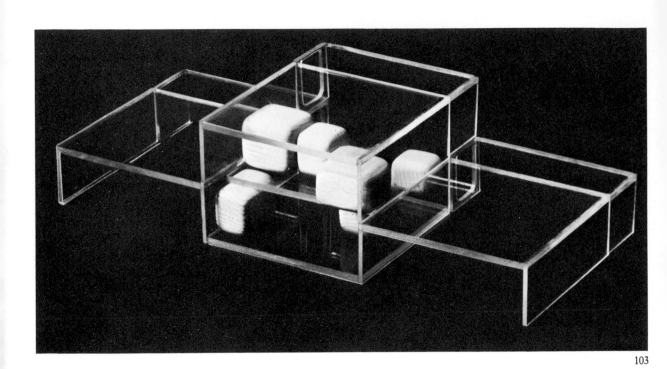

103

104

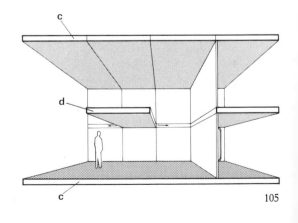

105

103–108. Columbia University Full-Scale Mock-Up. The mock-up represents the solution for the dwelling unit 3E obtained by the aggregation of Frame Components of types (c, d). *103.* Schematic model showing Frame Components and Function Objects. *104.* Function Objects under construction in the Columbia University lab. *105.* Longitudinal section—perspective of the dwelling. *106–108.* Three dwelling layouts, 3E1, 3E2, 3E3. Above: Plans of the upper floors. Below: Plans of the lower floors.

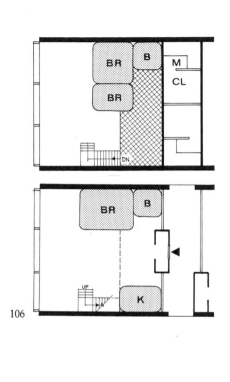

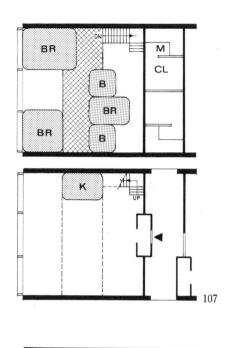

106

107

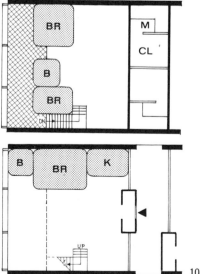

108

109–110. Views of the Columbia University Full-Scale Mock-Up.

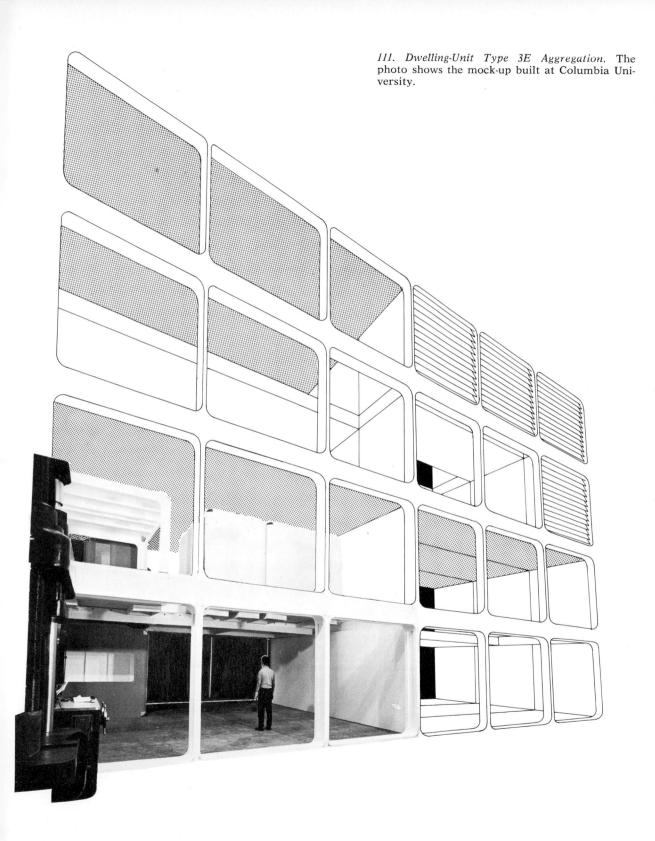

111. Dwelling-Unit Type 3E Aggregation. The photo shows the mock-up built at Columbia University.

112–113. Schematic Patterns. 112. Perspective of schematic pattern. The drawing illustrates horizontal, terraced, and vertical patterns. *113.* Section and perspective sketches of patterns obtained with Frame Components of System 3. Both the horizontal pattern and the terraced one are made of dwelling-unit type 3E.

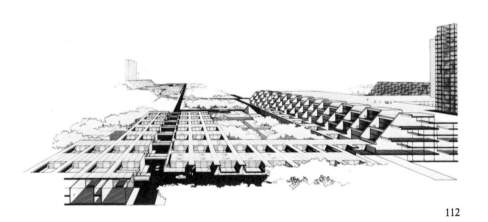

112

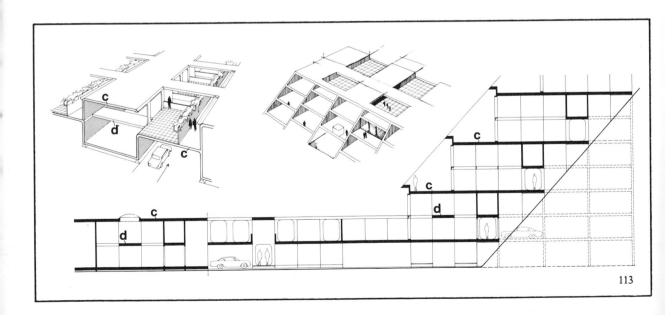

113

114–115. Schematic Patterns. 114. Perspective of schematic horizontal and terraced patterns made with dwelling-unit type 3E. *115.* Section showing horizontal and terraced pattern made with dwelling-unit type 3E.

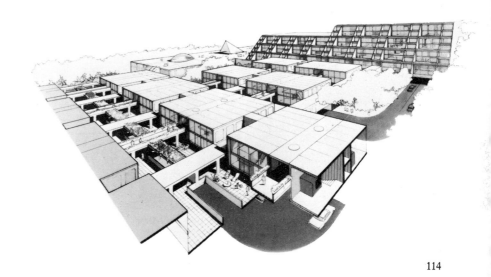

114

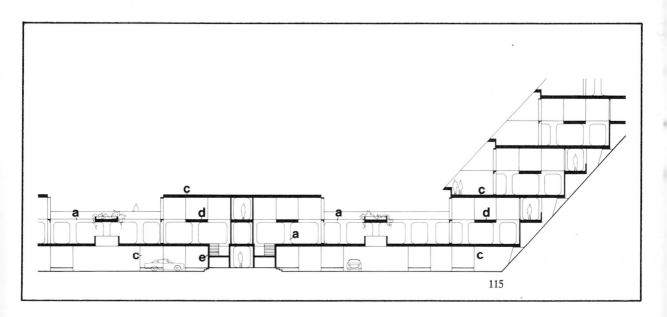

115

116–117. Schematic Patterns. 116. Horizontal and terraced patterns made with dwelling-unit type 3B. *117.* Sections showing horizontal pattern made with dwelling-unit type 3B and terraced pattern made with dwelling-unit type 3A. The sketches show the internal volume of dwelling unit 3B and the terraces of dwelling-unit type 3A.

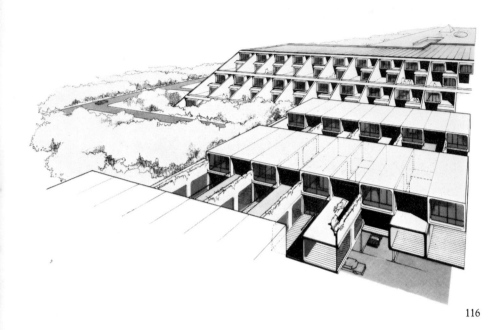

116

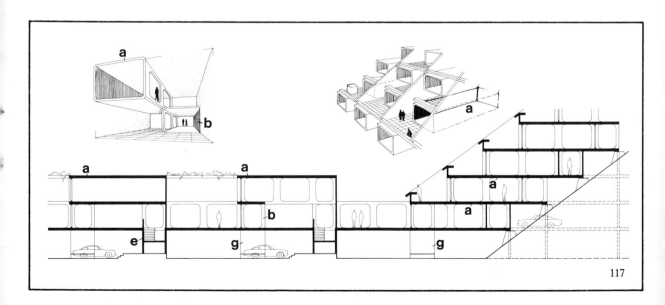

117

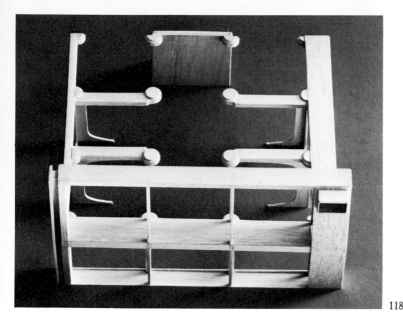

118

118. Mechanical Frame. Views of model.

119. Mechanical System. Drawing showing the outlets and connections.

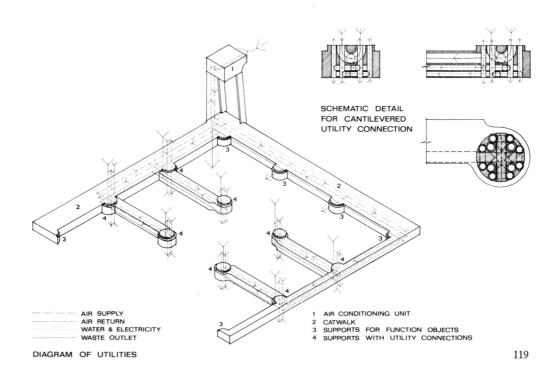

SCHEMATIC DETAIL
FOR CANTILEVERED
UTILITY CONNECTION

― ― ― AIR SUPPLY	1 AIR CONDITIONING UNIT
― ― ― AIR RETURN	2 CATWALK
·········· WATER & ELECTRICITY	3 SUPPORTS FOR FUNCTION OBJECTS
――――― WASTE OUTLET	4 SUPPORTS WITH UTILITY CONNECTIONS

DIAGRAM OF UTILITIES

119

120

120–122. Mechanical Frame. 120. Function Objects to be connected to the mechanical frame. *121.* Perspective of Function Object connected to the mechanical frame. A system based on the mechanical frame will allow several thousands of internal solutions. *122.* Plan of mechanical frame.

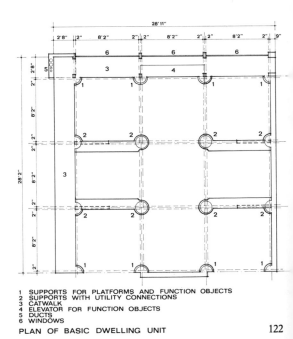

121

1 SUPPORTS FOR PLATFORMS AND FUNCTION OBJECTS
2 SUPPORTS WITH UTILITY CONNECTIONS
3 CATWALK
4 ELEVATOR FOR FUNCTION OBJECTS
5 DUCTS
6 WINDOWS

PLAN OF BASIC DWELLING UNIT

122

123

124

123–125. *Function Objects. 123.* Function Objects in a spatial relationship. *124.* Mechanical frame model with Function Objects. *125.* Plan of typical Function Objects.

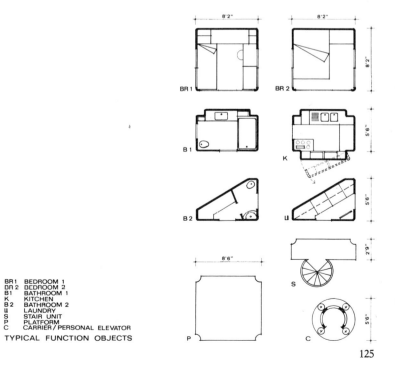

BR1 BEDROOM 1
BR 2 BEDROOM 2
B1 BATHROOM 1
K KITCHEN
B2 BATHROOM 2
u LAUNDRY
S STAIR UNIT
P PLATFORM
C CARRIER / PERSONAL ELEVATOR

TYPICAL FUNCTION OBJECTS

125

126. Function Objects. The sketches show a geometrical relationship among Function Objects of a possible system. Many elaborate geometries can be applied, and, consequently, many forms and sizes of Function Objects can be obtained. The mechanical frame has to be designed in accordance with the shapes of Function Objects.

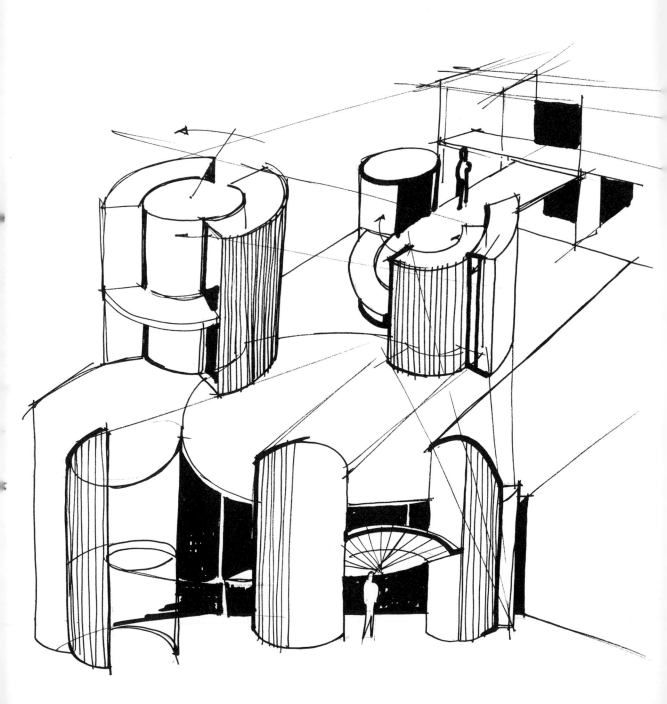

X.

The Forms of Freedom on an Urban Scale

Production City and Nature City ·
Implementation ·
Technical Appendix

The future environment will derive from the image of the mass culture in the form of Equipotential Space. The quality of life we want and the quality of architecture we attain will grow from the same needs and responses.

The geometry of Equipotential Space, taking any form so long as it accounts for the relationships between personal and shared needs, is therefore a non-finite, dynamic geometry of continuously interrelated volumes. The possibility of making Equipotential Space into any form, as desired or required, is the guarantee of respect for the dimension of freedom.

The basic question remains: In the future, to what extent will the environment allow individual thought to develop and participate? Our answer is that only when the principle of freedom is accepted can each participating individual influence all decisions. If we could not defend this principle, technology would certainly destroy our entire cultural heritage; it could become a medium of total oppression were we dogmatically to apply a technocratic order.

For these reasons, even though all the components and objects we would use in urban compositions would be products of technology and come from assembly lines, the final order of the composition should not be predetermined but should come out of freedom and individual participation. This order may be artistic—even metaphysical—or purely empiricist when a utilitarian solution is required.

The works of technology and of art, both expressions of conscious human thought, must find a common ground. This common ground can grow without limits in the freedom of a participatory democracy.

In this context, we visualize two extreme solutions, both built with the same assembly-line components and each representing one of the two conflicting ideals in our cultural heritage—the urban image and the pastoral one.

The first we will call "Production City" and imagine as a hive (*Figs. 127–29*). Economically determining the optimum total volume and the sizes of its interior spaces will minimize the lengths of communication links, power losses, and exterior surfaces. It will be efficient, productive, full of action, and highly communal and social.

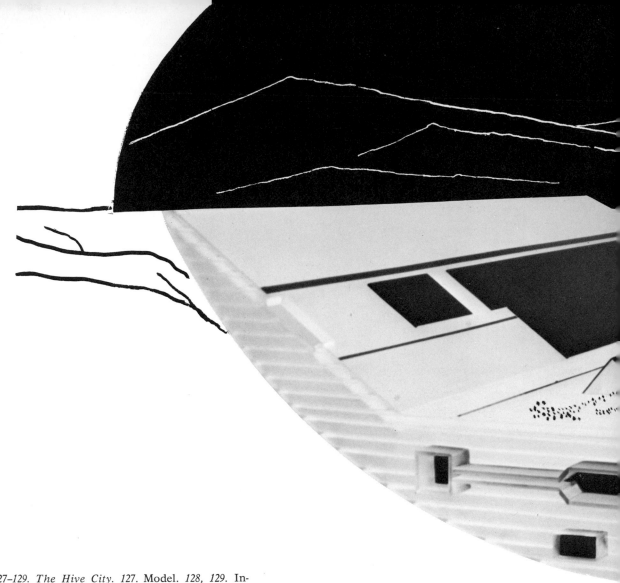

127–129. *The Hive City.* 127. Model. *128, 129.* Interface between buildings and ground.

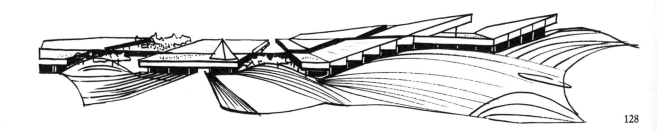

128

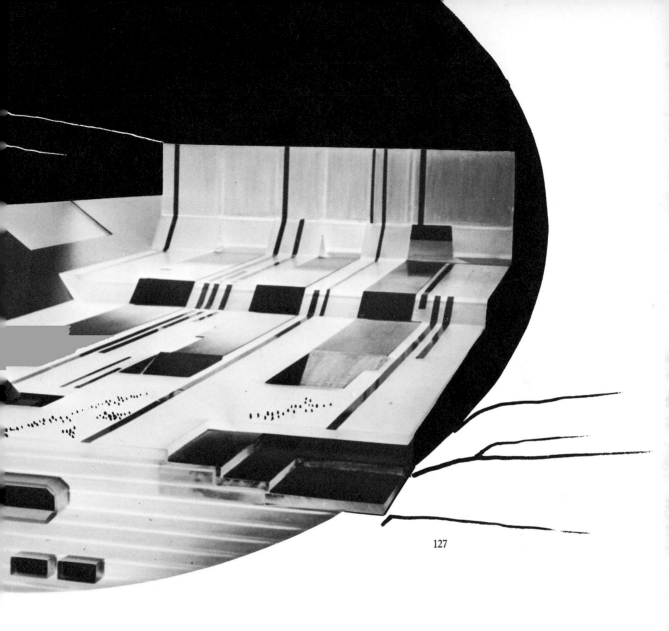

127

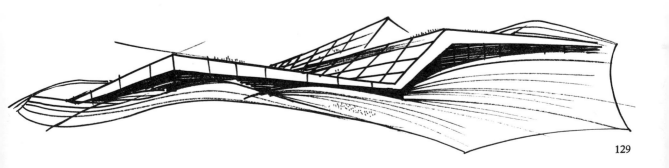

129

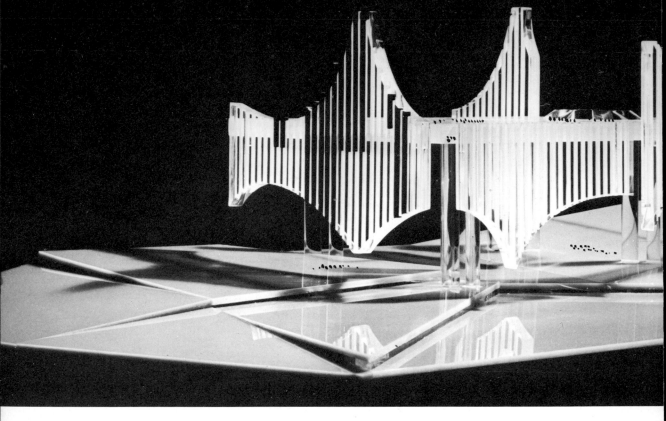

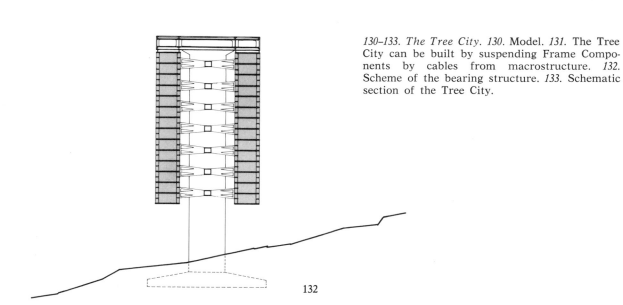

130–133. The Tree City. 130. Model. *131.* The Tree City can be built by suspending Frame Components by cables from macrostructure. *132.* Scheme of the bearing structure. *133.* Schematic section of the Tree City.

132

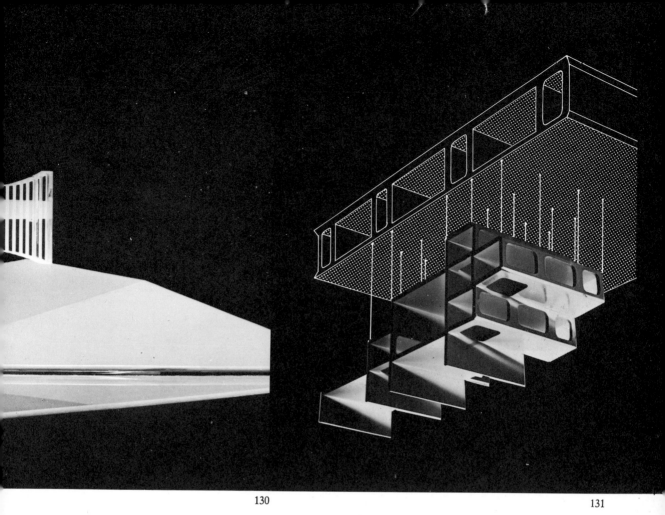

130

131

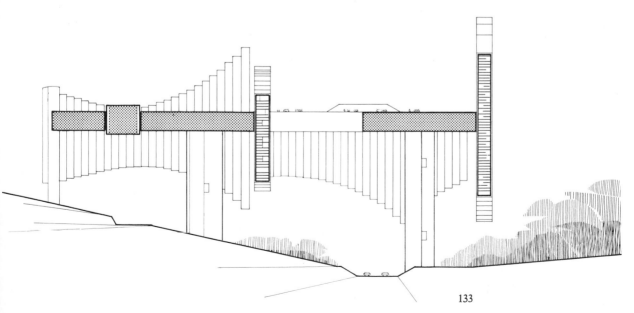

133

The second, we will call "Nature City" (*Figs. 130–33*) and imagine it as a tree. Like a tree, it is arranged for as much exposure as possible to light and air. Detached from the ground, it allows the natural environment to grow and thrive in concert with itself. It could be a city of contemplation and the simple enjoyment of physical well-being. In touch with the world around, it knows the luxury of a more leisurely pattern of life.

These two extremes are in fact not antithetical, but should be coexisting patterns in terms of total needs. If they expressed opposing views of life, the continuity of experience that should be the hallmark of the mass society could not exist.

Continuity and sameness are not identical. The relationships between differences in any society are more important than the differences themselves. If we considered that all functional needs were similar and that one particular geometry and density could answer them, we could imagine spreading out over the surface of our land in a broad wave of blandness, building neither usable cities nor preserving our natural environment, destroying both man and his world.

This bleak prospect has become the mythical "curse of technology." And yet this is not an inevitable outcome; indeed, this bland sameness is not the natural product of the creative application of technology, nor could it exist in Equipotential Space. The dilemma of the standard is resolved in the standard of response possible through technology.

In any city, then, if there is to be the continuity of the life we hope to foster, there will be concurrent patterns of both the hive and the tree. In the life of any man there will be a mixture of the needs from which each pattern is derived, and it is in the physical fabric of his cities that these needs must be answered. The necessary efficiency of the particular response will be determined by the economic situation of the individual, family, organization, and community.

The standard will have to reflect the total spectrum of needs in the personal, familial, social, and political life of men. Equipotential Space will allow the most highly particularized solutions to specific needs on all these levels, at specific places and specific times. It will be a mix of high and low density, man and nature, science and art, fact and fantasy. The primary differences among men will then be in their individual choices of mix and not in the difference of standards available to them.

Technical Appendix

Equipotential Space can be used as a tool to achieve not only all the possibilities of the patterns but primarily the most economical solutions.

The use of Equipotential Space as a method of analysis helps a great deal to clarify all the aspects of architecture. In this process, it becomes apparent that many features of buildings that are believed to derive only from the sensitivity of the designer can be more properly related by the order of a system.

A brief analysis of a number of projects designed without the use of Equipotential Space (*Figs. 134–47*) demonstrates the need for a methodology that could unify volumes and the structures necessary to contain them. In so doing, we would avoid all those spatial interruptions due to pretentious and individualistic edifices visible in the streets of the contemporary city.

A research project on apartment buildings was carried out in 1958 as an attempt to resolve the age-old problem of spatial continuity at ground level, which architecture almost always destroys in cities (*Figs. 134–37*). The platform, which contains from 150 to 200 apartments, is elevated above the ground and rests on structural cores in which garages and other facilities are arranged. The access road to the building goes underground to maintain the continuity of the terrain.

134

135

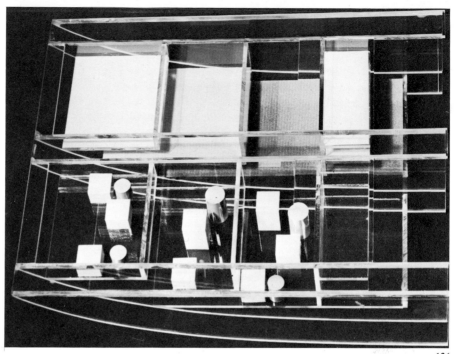

136

134–137. *Horizontal Apartment Unit.* Research project. About 200 apartments are contained in the horizontal pattern raised above the ground (*134, 135*). The horizontal pattern can be built with the assemblage of Frame Components and Function Objects (*136, 137*).

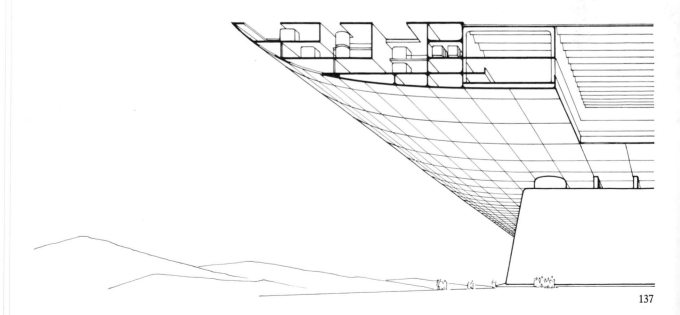

137

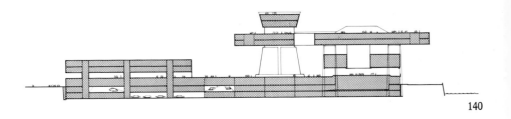

140

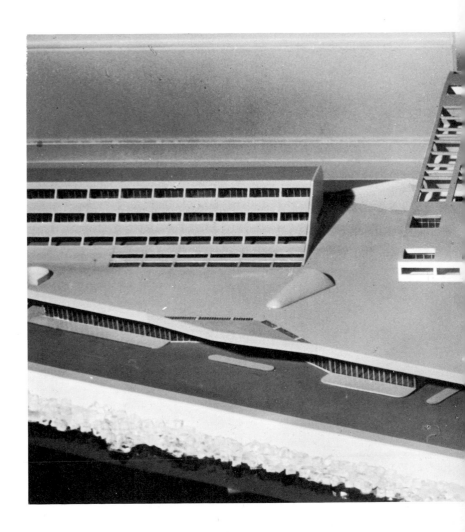

141

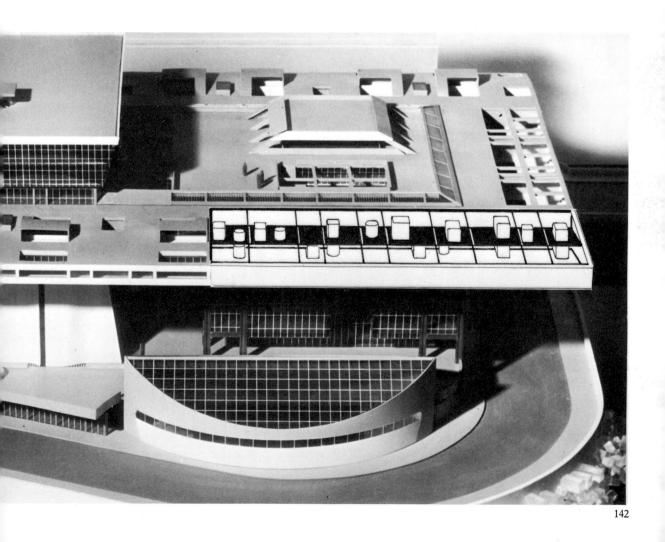

142

137

143–144. Cultural Center of University College of Cape Coast, Cape Coast, Ghana. 1964. Section and view of model. Another application of Function Objects and Frame Components to an elaborated building shape.

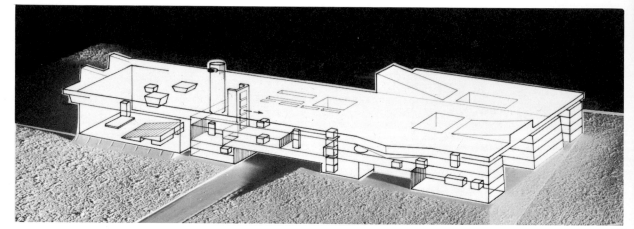

143

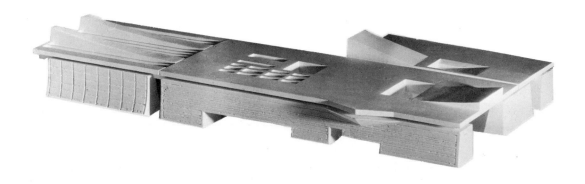

144

145–147. Government Office Buildings and Trade Center, Kampala, Uganda. 1970. View of building under construction, section, and model. The components of this building were built in Italy and transported to Uganda to be assembled by local labor.

145

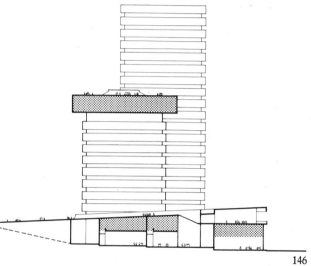

146

147

At present, we have reason to fear that the world may remain divided in two: a world affluent enough to afford the luxury of supporting both freedom and development, and a world of the poor that cannot afford either. A bridge must be built between these two worlds. Technology can build such a bridge. It is a medium large enough in scope and creative enough in application to meet the demands of all countries and all cultures. In every country, architecture can be produced through the application of advanced technology. The increasing use of technology and industrialization is an irreversible trend. The major powers of East and West and all the developing countries either use—or aspire to use—industrialization in construction.

As our new environment is built, a new industry and a new market will grow simultaneously. We foresee a future market similar to that of our present automobile industry, its related infrastructure of highways and complementary businesses.

The traditional processes of architecture are no longer relevant on the scale of the mass society, and a new process has to be established in a short time. The architects' contribution will be to create a format in which all the diverse efforts of designers, producers, and consumers can find a common expression. The problem is great and the solution difficult to reach, but the concurrent searches of designers and producers will merge into the large-scale industrialized production of buildings. This process will take many years to become articulated at every level of participation but will finally make full use of all available creative human energies.

This book has described a process in which the transmission of information and experience is continuous and total among all the participants and avoids unique, separatist, and personalistic approaches.

This new process must be able to adapt to any new developments in life-styles that accompany the rapid population-growth and urbanization. Although, as we have seen, the dwelling unit will not necessarily fit any but the present Western model of society, and although the family structure may change in the future, we feel that the basic principles of Equipotential Space can be universal and flexible in application.

Conclusion

We have spoken of the dilemma of standards. We cannot know how much of Western culture will survive in the process of developing and applying these standards. High quality of life is what distinguishes today's Western culture and political system from any other culture or ideology. To remain a valid model for the emerging world, Western culture must be able to develop a process in which that distinctive quality, fulfills the demands of many. The development of this process is a fundamental necessity for the West—a matter of survival that can be the moral commitment we need. The implementation of this commitment must become our image of the future.